Waterloo Ontario Book 3 in Colour Photos, Saving Our History One Photo at a Time

Photography
by Barbara Raué
updated 2016

Series Name:
Cruising Ontario

Book 116: Waterloo Book 3,
and Breslau

Cover photo: view of Silver Lake

Series Name: Cruising Ontario
Saving Our History One Photo at a Time
in colour photos

Other Books by Barbara Raue

Coins of Gold

Arrows, Indians and Love

The Life and Times of Barbara
Volume 1: Inventions That Have Enhanced My Life
Volume 2: Entertainment That I Have Enjoyed
Volume 3: East Coast Trips
Volume 4: Olympics Have Always Intrigued Me
Volume 5: Wonders of the World
Volume 6: Caribbean Cruises We Have Enjoyed
Volume 7: Animals
Volume 8: Storms and Other Major Disasters in My Lifetime
Volume 9: Wars, Terrorist Attacks and Major Disasters

The Cromwell Family Book

Laura Secord Discovered

Daddy Where Are You?

Visit Barbara's website to view all of her books
http://barbararaue.ca

Waterloo is a city in Southern Ontario. The Conestogo Parkway and Highway 8 connect Waterloo with Kitchener, Cambridge, Highway 7/8, and Highway 401. Waterloo shares several of its north-south arterial roads with neighboring Kitchener.

Waterloo was built on land that was part of a parcel of 675,000 acres assigned in 1784 to the Iroquois alliance that made up the League of Six Nations as a reward for their loyalty to the British during the American Revolution as well as to compensate for lost lands in New York State. Almost immediately, the native groups began to sell some of the land. Between 1796 and 1798, 93,000 acres were sold through a Crown Grant to Richard Beasley, with the Six Nations Indians continuing to hold the mortgage on the lands.

The first immigrants to the area were Mennonites from Pennsylvania. They bought deeds to land parcels from Beasley and began moving into the area in 1804. The following year, a group of twenty-six Mennonites pooled resources to purchase all of the unsold land from Beasley and discharge the mortgage held by the Six Nations Indians.

The Mennonites divided the land into smaller lots; two lots initially owned by Abraham Erb became the central core of Waterloo. Erb built a sawmill on Beaver, now Laurel, Creek in 1808 and in 1816 built the area's first grist mill which farmers from miles around used to grind their wheat into flour, a very important staple. The edges of a beaver pond were raised to provide enough water to power the grist mill. This pond formed what is now Silver Lake. Workers dug a sixteen-foot-wide ditch, called a millrace, which channeled water down the slope to make it flow faster from the pond to the mill. The water flowed into a wooden flume which directed the water to the waterwheel which was eighteen feet in diameter and was located at the back of the mill. From the mill, the water flowed down a tail race to Beaver Creek.

The gristmill remained in continuous operation for 111 years. The pioneers often had a long wait for their flour and sometimes had to spend the night. Other businesses began to locate near the booming mills, providing important services to visiting farmers. Farmers would go to the blacksmith, have their harnesses repaired, or visit the general store while they waited for their flour.

In 1816, the new township was named after Waterloo, Belgium, the site of the Battle of Waterloo, which had ended the Napoleonic Wars in Europe. After that war, the area became a popular destination for German immigrants. By the 1840s, German settlers were the dominant segment of the population. Many Germans settled in the small hamlet to the southeast of Waterloo. In their honor, the village was named Berlin in 1833 (renamed to Kitchener in 1916). Berlin was chosen as the site of the seat for the County of Waterloo in 1853.

The inhabitants established Waterloo as an important industrial and commercial center. The village had a council chamber, fire hall, post office, library, and four steam-powered factories, including the Granite Mills and Distillery which became the Seagram Company.

The Grand River flows southward along the east side of the city. Its most significant tributary within the city is Laurel Creek, whose source lies just to the west of the city limits and its mouth just to the east, and crosses much of the city's central areas including the University of Waterloo lands and Waterloo Park; it flows under the uptown area in a culvert. In the west end of the city, the Waterloo Moraine provides over 300,000 people in the region with drinking water. Much of the gently hilly Waterloo Moraine underlies existing developed areas.

The railway came to Waterloo in 1886. The first frame station for the Grand Trunk Railway (later Canadian National) was built on Queen Street (now called Regina). The main tracks ended at the station and a spur line was built across King Street to serve Union Mills. A new rail line was built in 1895 to extend the railway to Elmira.

The Grand Trunk Railway bought a right-of-way to cross the millpond from William Snider. A wooden trestle bridge was built across the deepest part of the lake which required large amounts of earth fill to build the approaches. When the millpond was sold in 1917 to the Town of Waterloo by the Snider Estate, a pedestrian walkway was added beside the railway tracks so that people could access Waterloo Park.

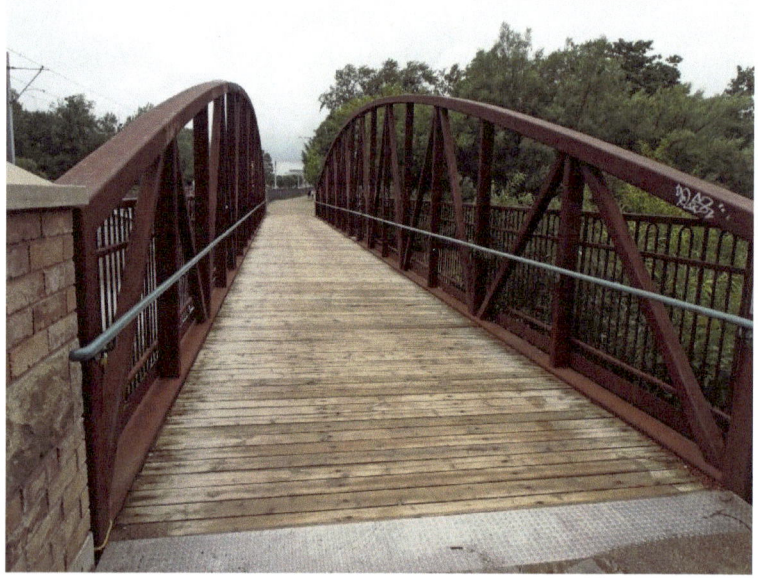

The Globe Furniture Company moved from Walkerville to Waterloo in 1910. It was merged with an existing company owned by E.F. Seagram known as the Toronto/Waterloo Furniture Company. The hand-carved door is a fine example of their work. The Globe Furniture was a company of cabinetmakers and skilled carpenters known for their artistic, neo-Gothic style wood carvings. They provided furnishings for schools, churches, scientific laboratories, and seats for theatre. The Globe Company created a carved impression of *The Last Supper* for over thirty churches throughout the world. The Globe Furniture Company office building still stands at the end of Canbar Street.

In 1853 Charles Mueller came to Waterloo from Germany and worked as a cooper for the Hespeler Randall and Roos Distillery before setting up his own business on Queen Street South in 1872, The Mueller Cooperage. As a skilled cooper, he could make twelve barrels per week, entirely by hand. White oak was cut into thin strips called staves. Once cut, the staves remained outside for a year to dry before being fitted into shape. Barrels were held together without glue. Steam was used to soften and shape the staves. Barrels from the Mueller Cooperage were used by the nearby distillery and brewery. In 1906, Mueller built a larger cooperage on Erb Street West installing modern machinery to reduce the manual labor. By 1916, the cooperage was making one thousand barrels per day.

At its peak, the Seagram Distillery had over 650,000 barrels of whiskey maturing for up to twelve years in its warehouses. Barrels were also shipped to Scotland, Jamaica, and Puerto Rico. Other barrels were sold for shipping vinegar, fresh water, pickles, preserved meats, and hardware supplies such as nails. In 1920, the business was sold to the Seagram family and the name changed to *Canada Barrels and Kegs*. In the 1950s, plastic containers and a line of fiberglass boats called the *Crestliner* were manufactured there. In 1973, the name of the business changed again to *Canbar*.

Breslau

Breslau is located at the junction of Highway 7 and Waterloo Regional Road 17 in the township of Woolwich and is separated from the city of Kitchener by the Grand River.

Breslau was established in 1850 when Joseph Erb built a dam, sawmill and a grist mill. The village was named after Breslau, the capital of Silesia, Germany. The history of the area dates farther back to the 1820s when members of the Cressman Mennonite Church began congregating in the homes of the early settlers. In 1834, the first meeting house was built in Waterloo County. The building was actually built in 1813 by Benjamin Eby and was moved to Breslau for the congregation. In 1856, a brick building replaced the log structure. In 1908, a larger church was built using bricks from the old church and in 1968, a new front entrance, pastor's study, and several Sunday School rooms were added. The name was changed to the Breslau Mennonite Church.

Table of Contents

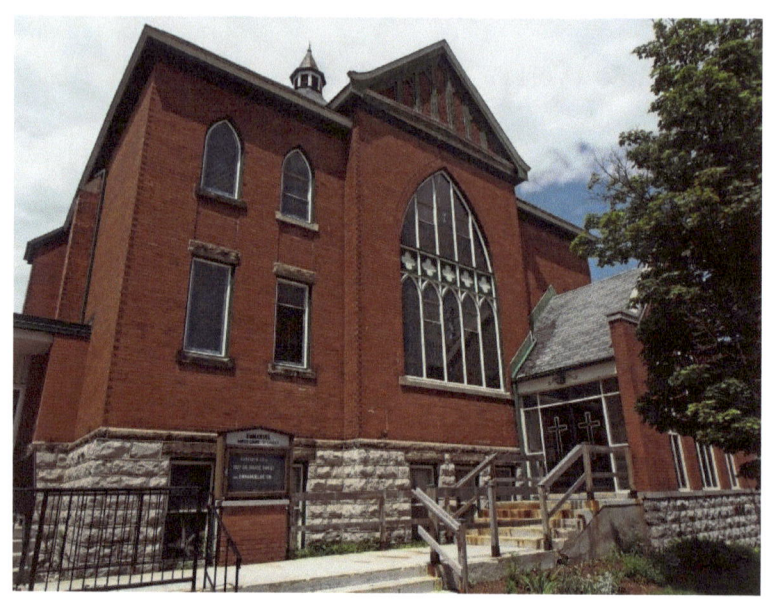

22 Bridgeport Road West – Emmanuel United Church

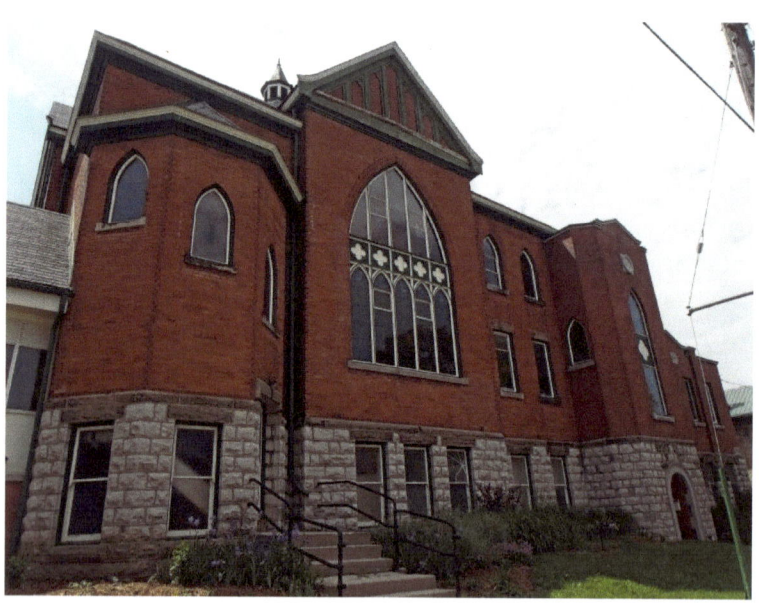

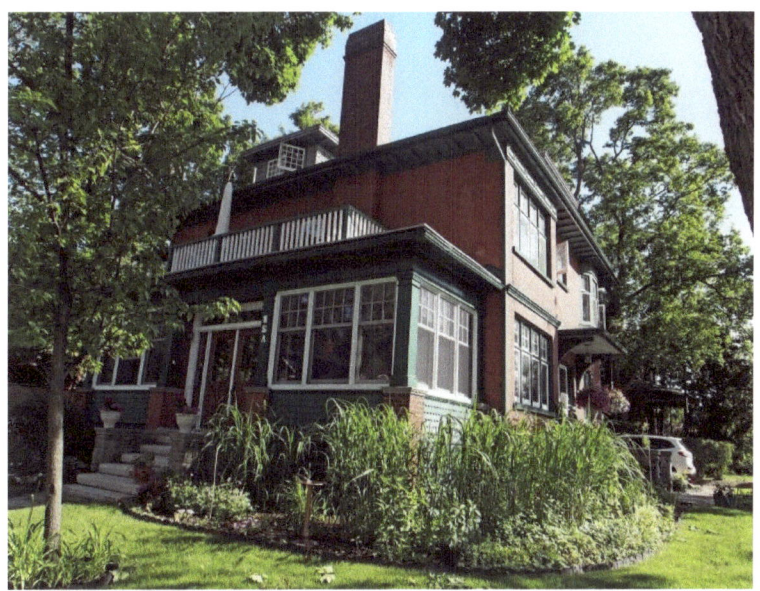

15 John Street East – Italianate, dormer in attic,
2nd floor balcony, enclosed verandah

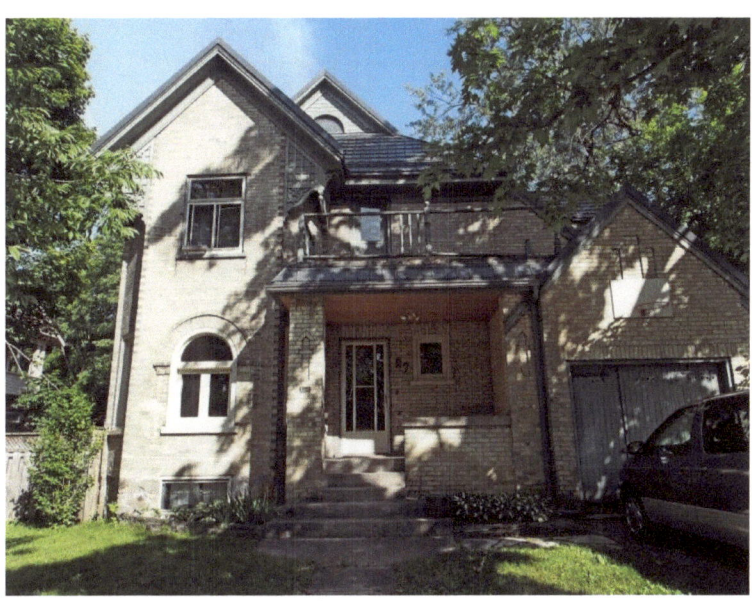

17 John Street East

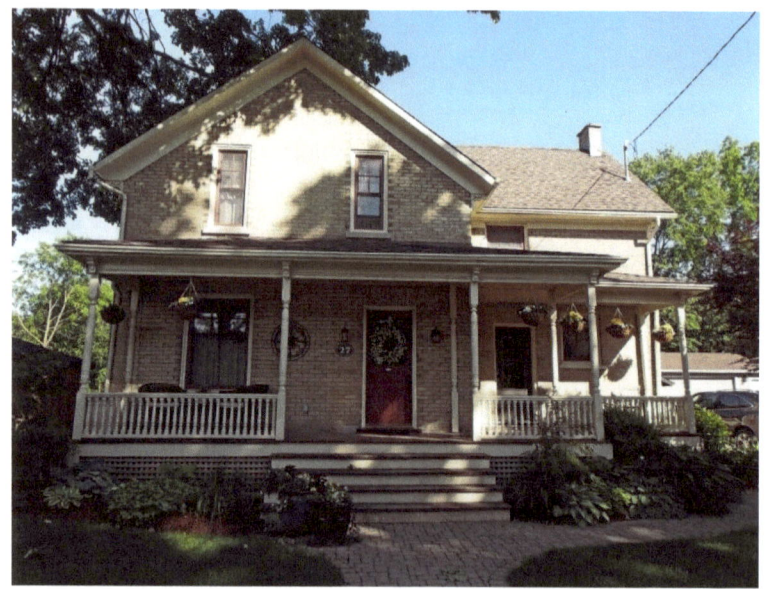

27 John Street East - vernacular

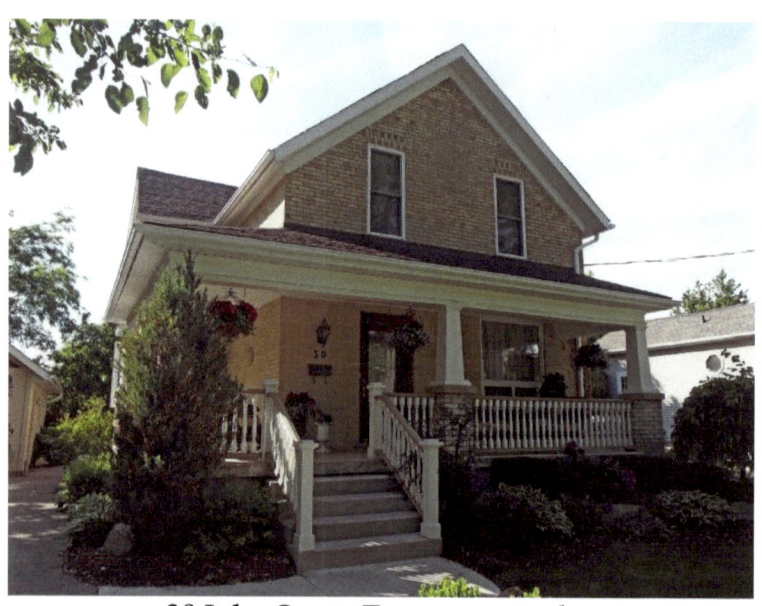

30 John Street East - vernacular

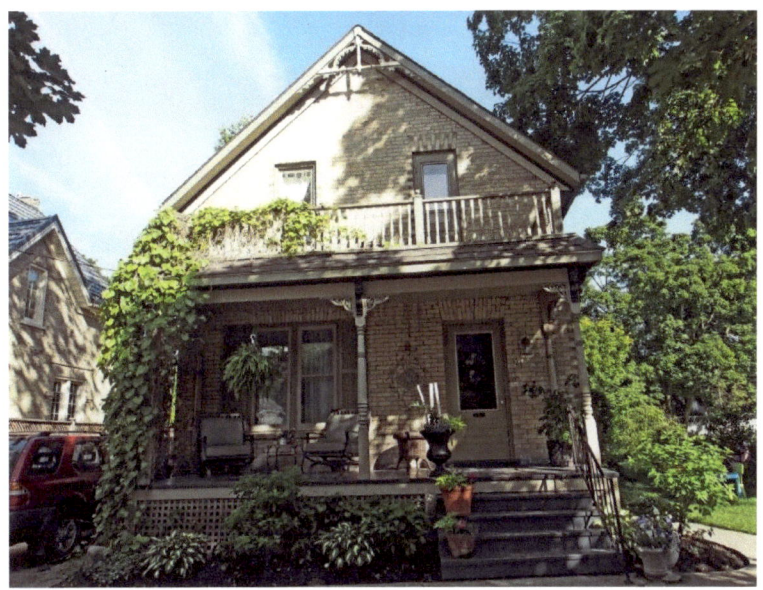

31 John Street East – Gothic - within peak of the gable
is a decorative arch with applied scrollwork,
spindles & circular piercing

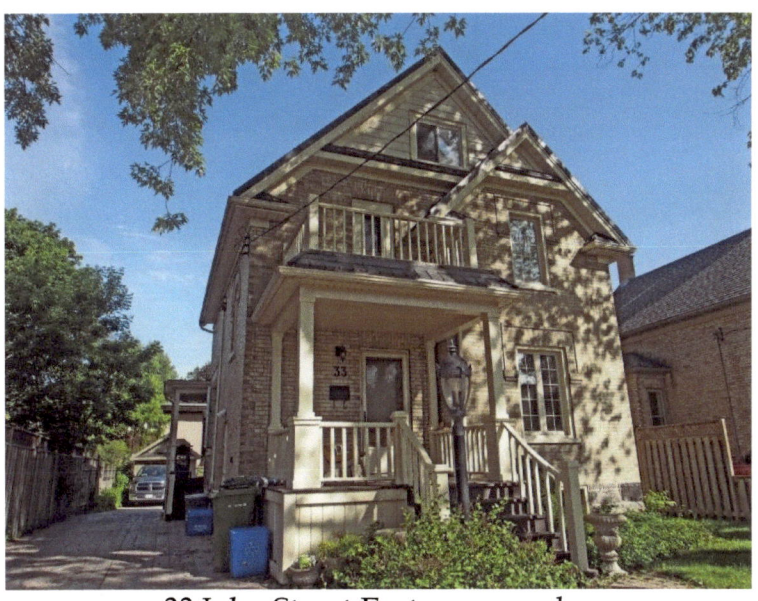

33 John Street East - vernacular

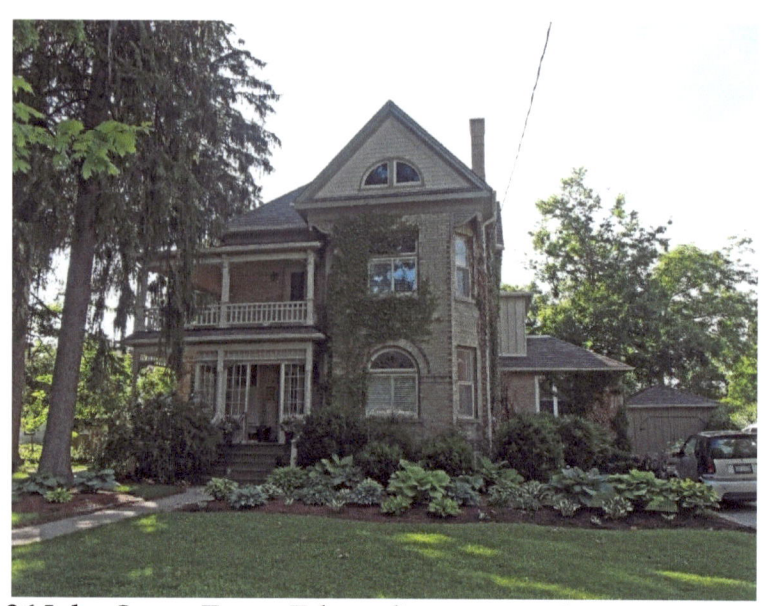

36 John Street East – Edwardian vernacular, two-storey
verandah, fretwork, Romanesque style window arch

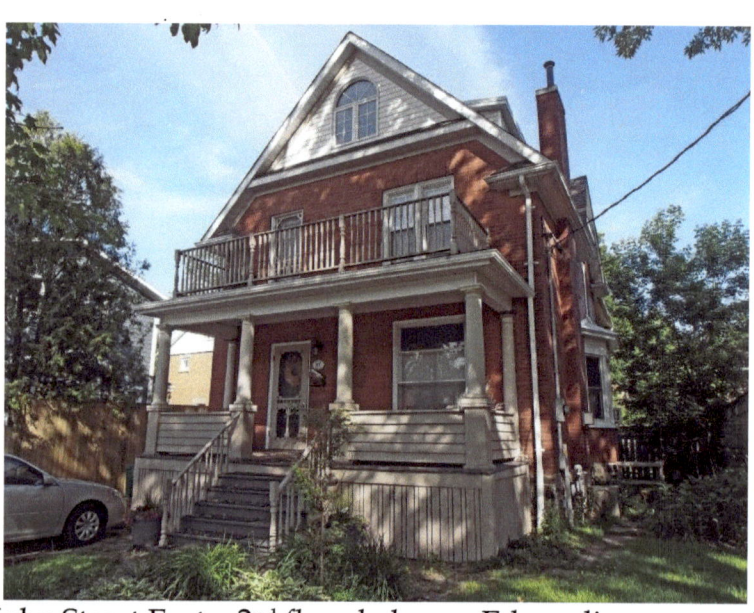

37 John Street East – 2nd floor balcony, Edwardian vernacular,
cornice return on gable

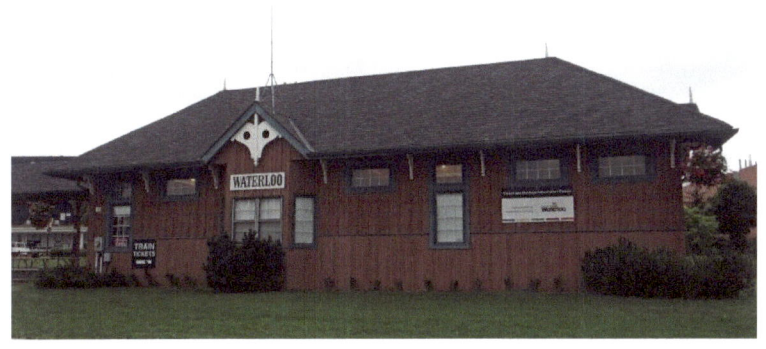

10 Father David Bauer Drive

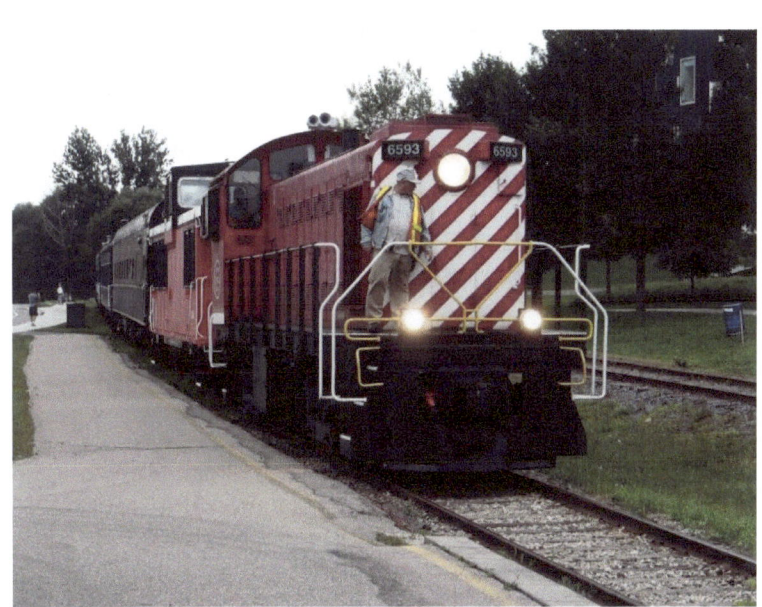

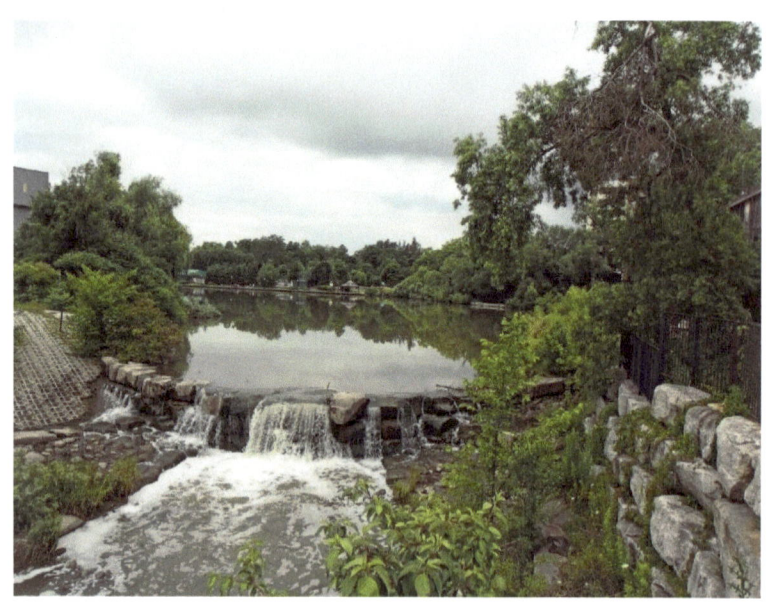

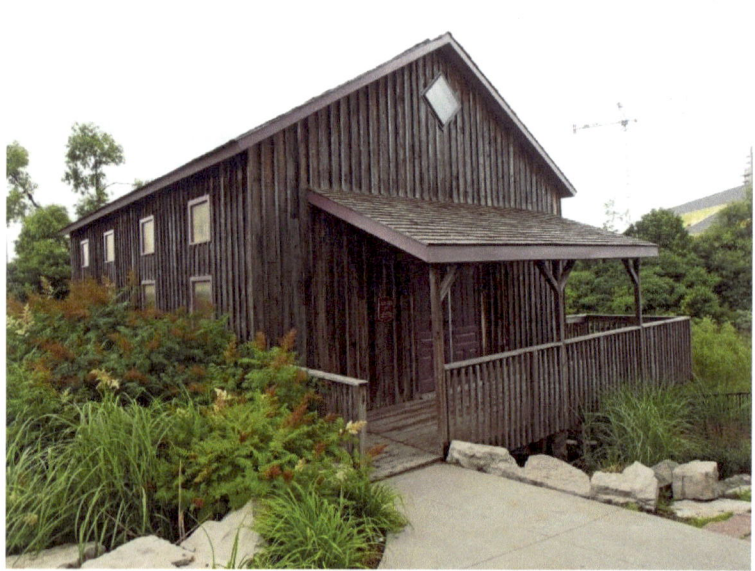

Abraham Erb built his grist mill in 1816 for grinding the local
farmers' wheat – this is a replica

Waterloo Park

On September 1, 1890, the Village of Waterloo acquired the 65-acre Jacob Eby farm to create its first park. The site included the Eby farmhouse, barn and orchard.

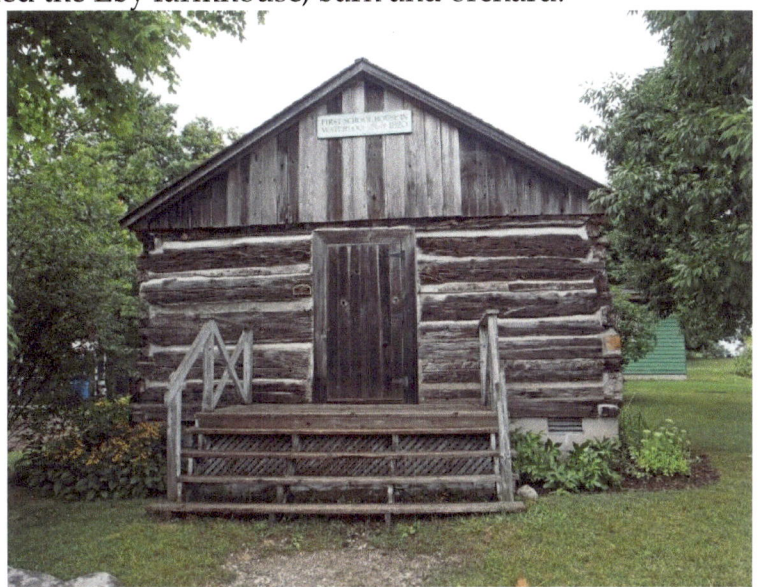

In 1894, the first log schoolhouse built in Waterloo was purchased and moved to Waterloo Park.

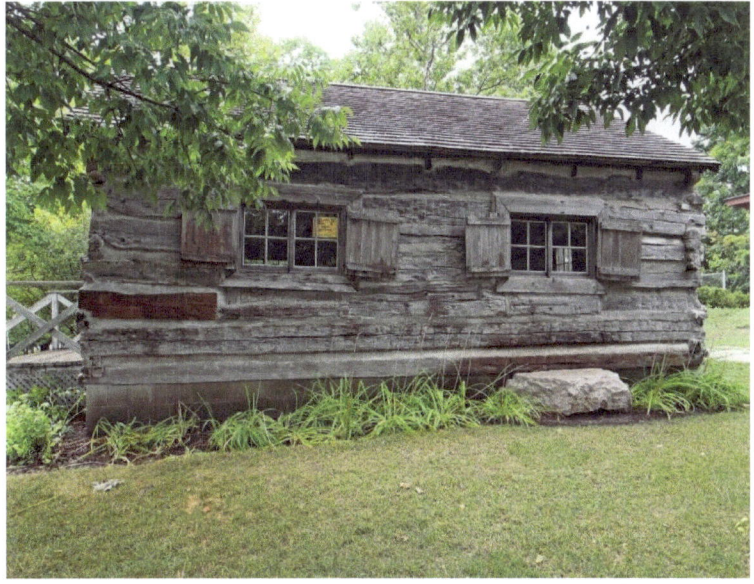

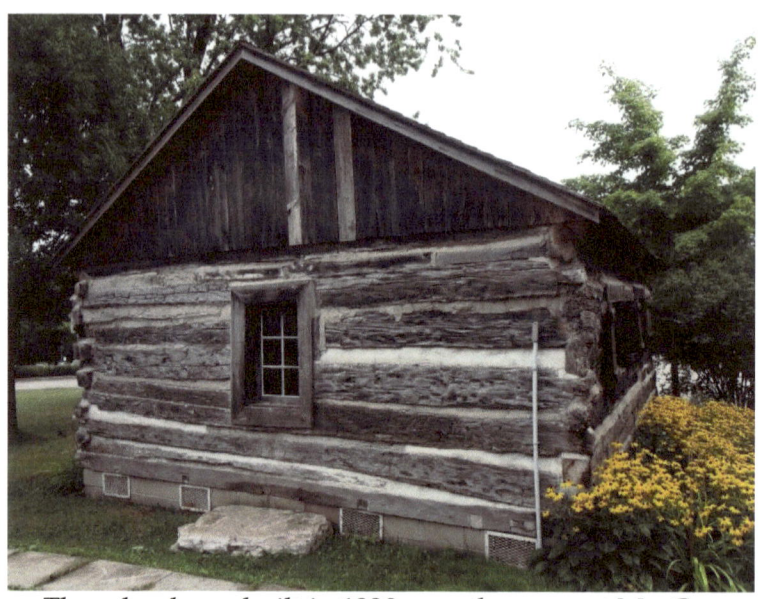

The school was built in 1820 near the present MacGregor Senior Public School.

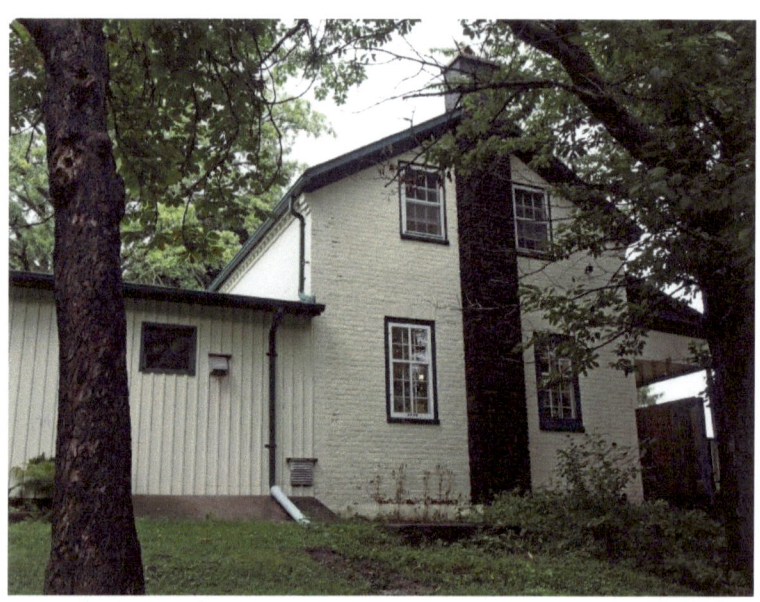

Eby Farmhouse – Waterloo Pottery Workshop

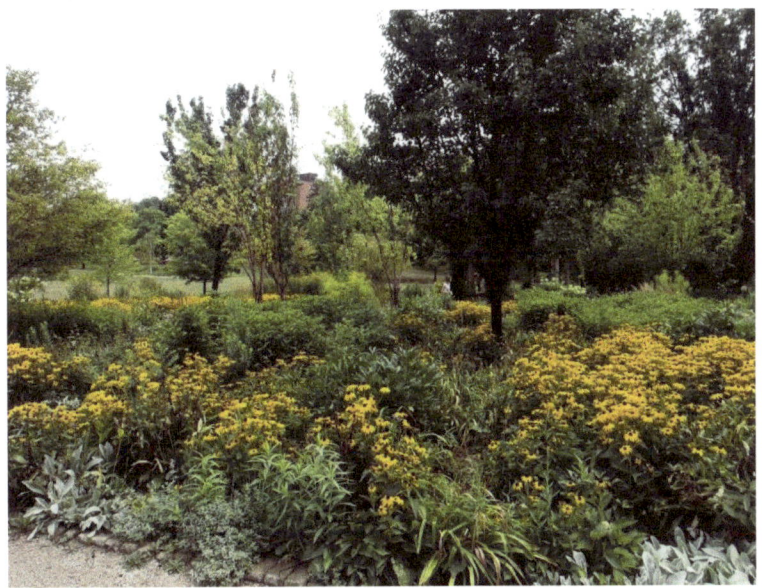

    Creating parkland out of farmland required extensive landscaping. In 1891, two thousand maple, elm and basswood trees were planted in rows and groves to create picnic areas, walkways and drives. The following year six hundred more trees were planted.

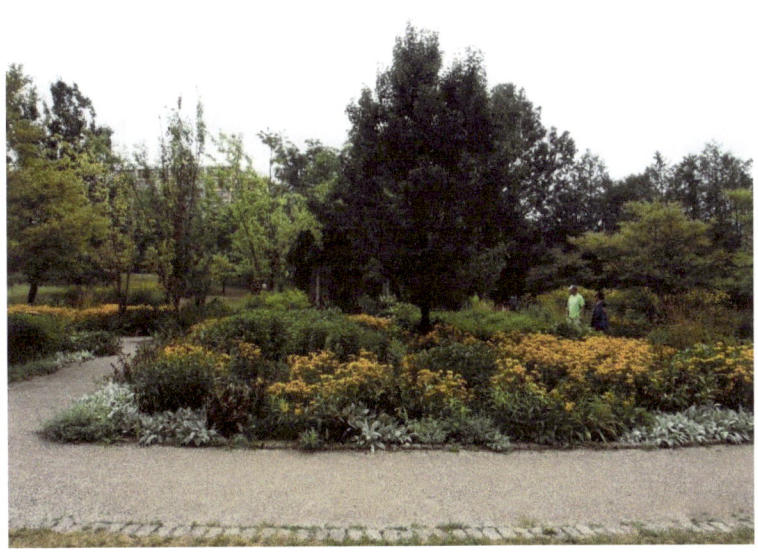

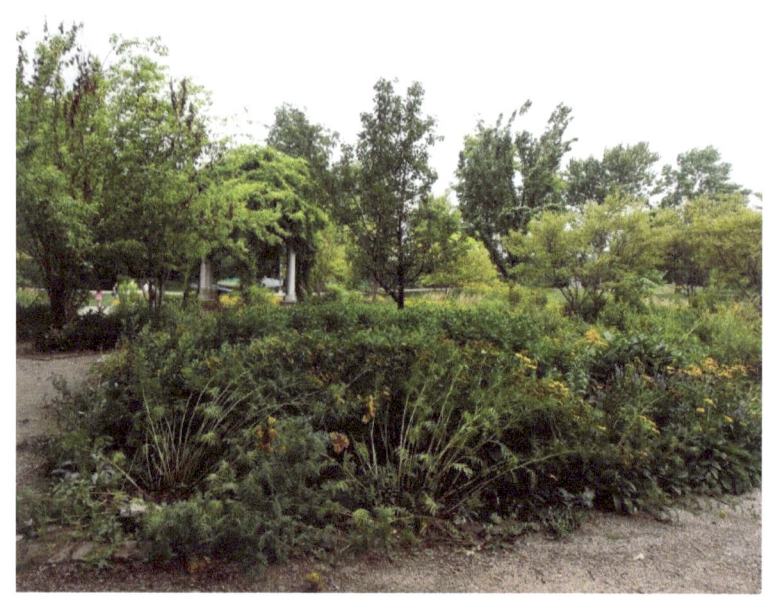

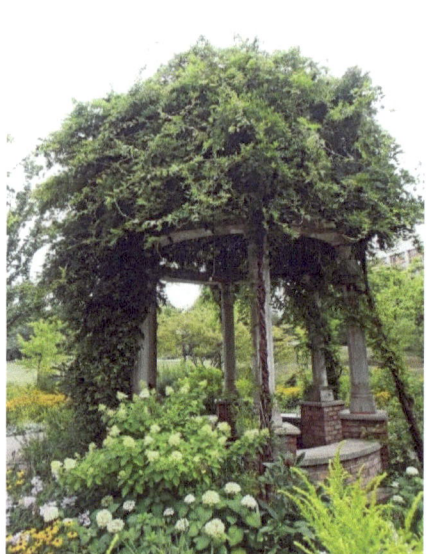

Pergola

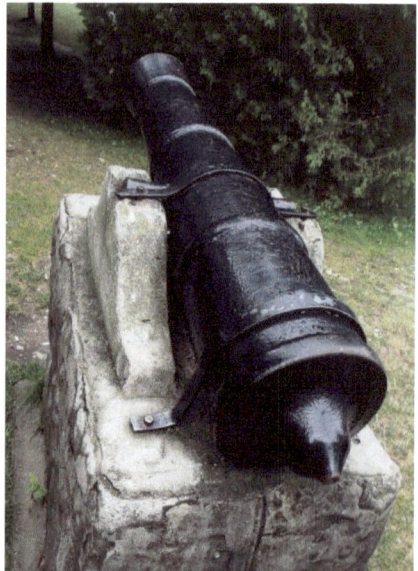

Cannon

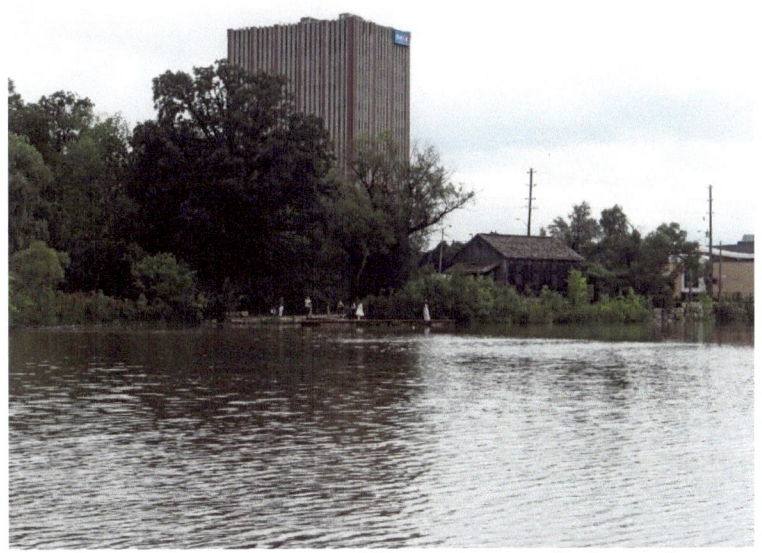

Silver Lake view – wedding pictures being taken

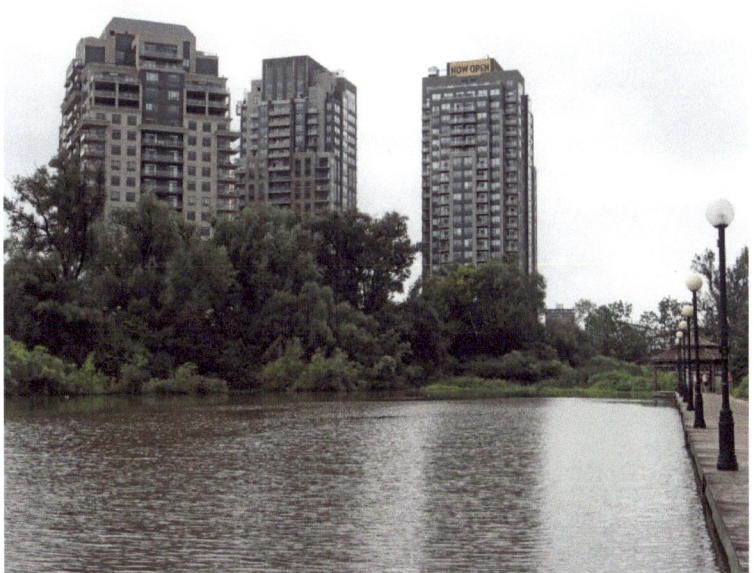

Silver Lake view

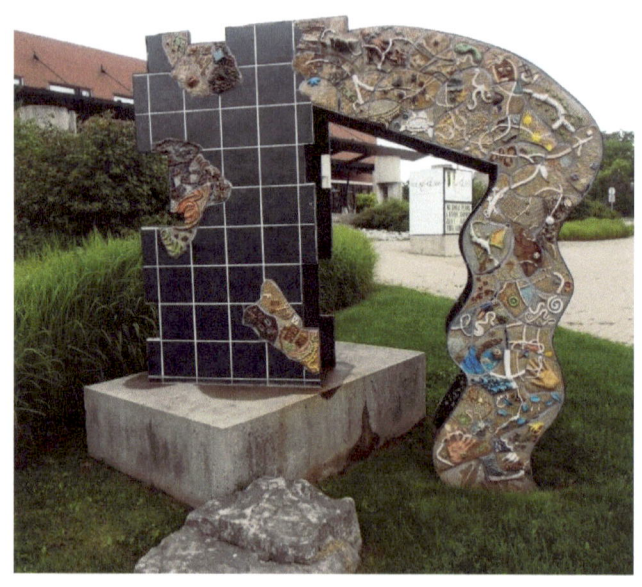

25 Caroline Street North – The Clay and Glass Gallery

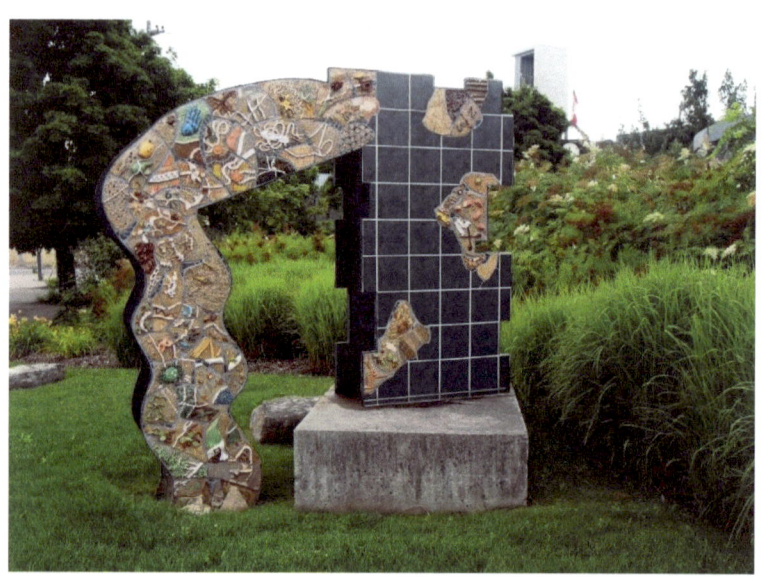

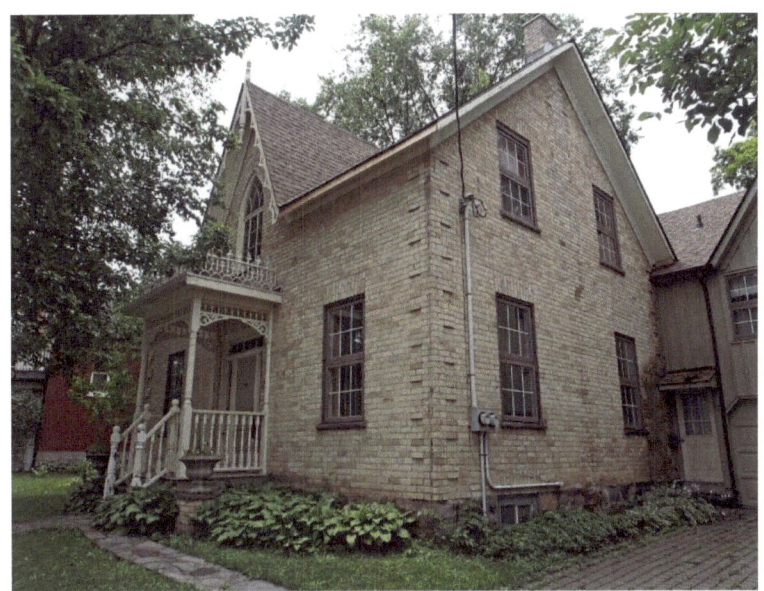

15 Euclid Avenue – Gothic Revival, bargeboard trim on gable with finial, Gothic window in gable; iron cresting above porch; corner quoins

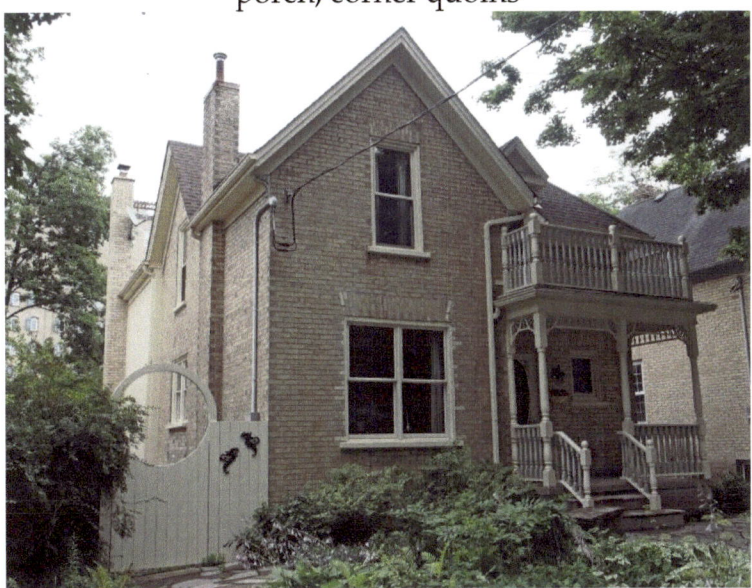

Euclid Avenue – Gothic – 2nd floor balcony, turned verandah supports with delicate spindles

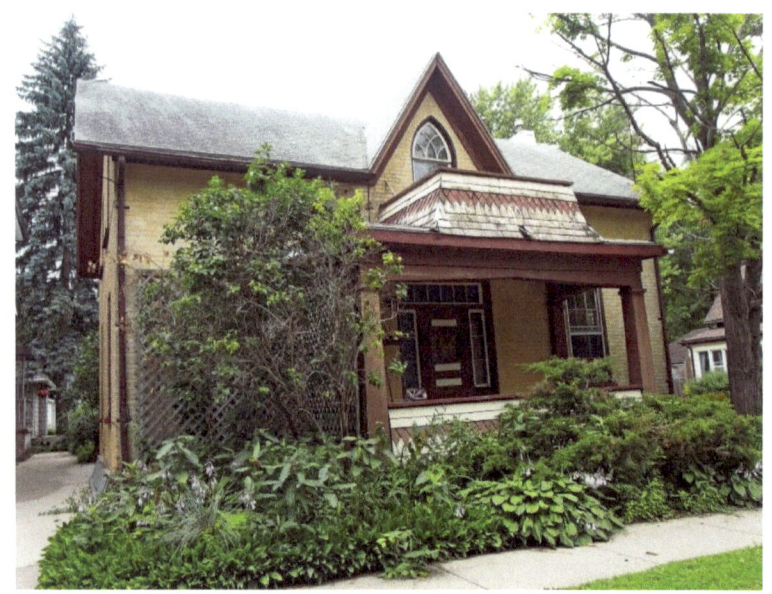

27 Euclid Avenue – Gothic Revival

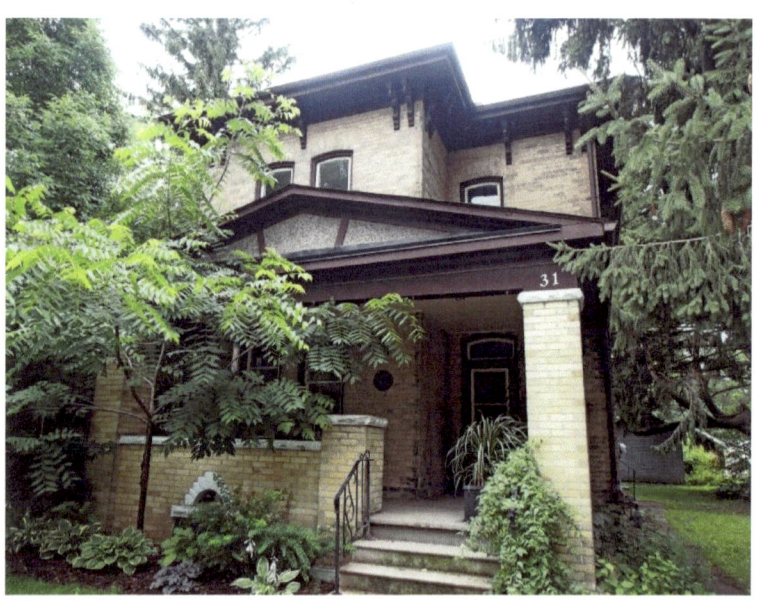

31 Euclid Avenue – Italianate – cornice brackets, pediment

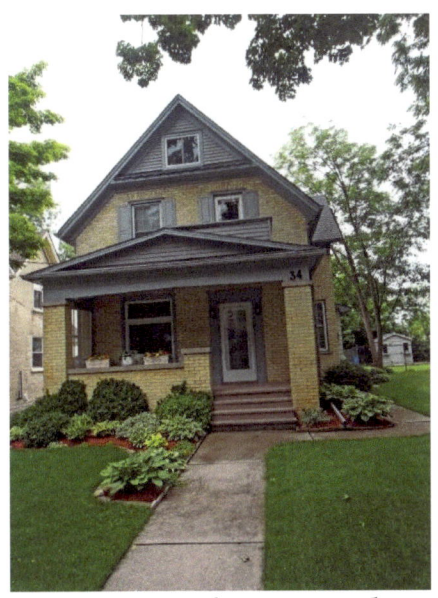

34 Euclid Avenue – Gothic vernacular, pediment

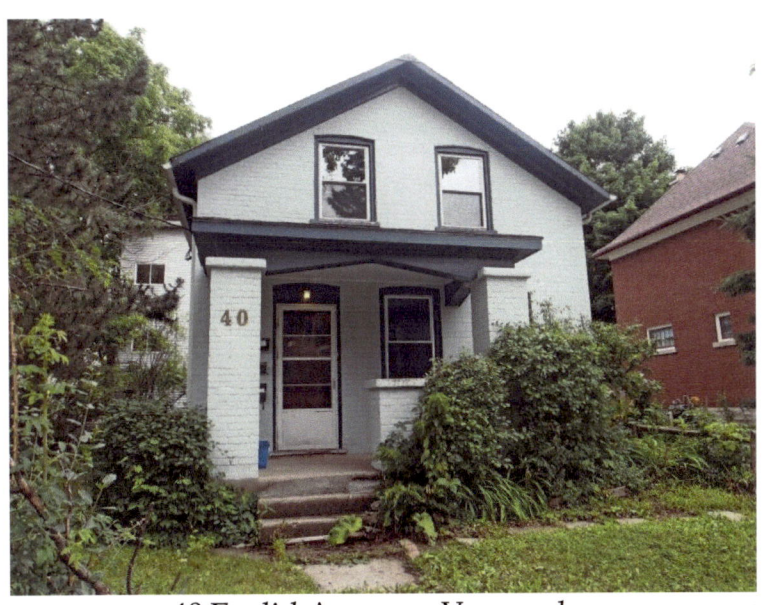

40 Euclid Avenue - Vernacular

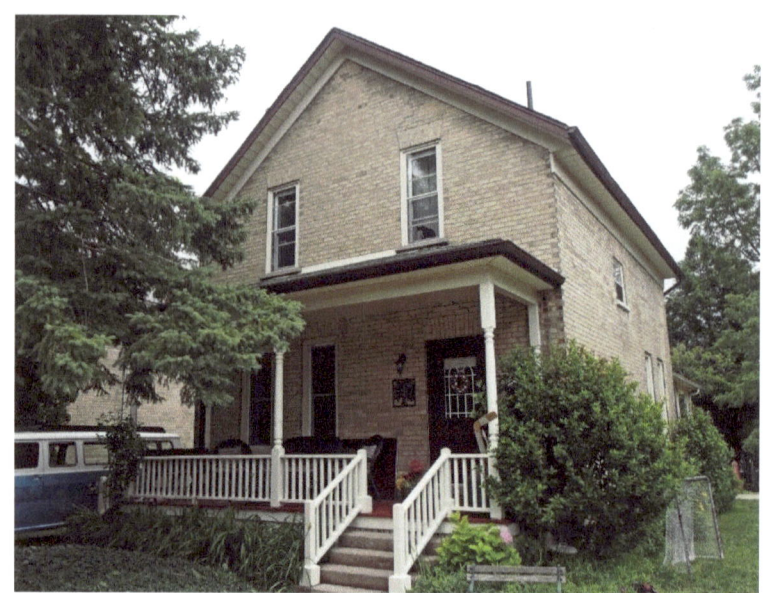

54 Euclid Avenue - Vernacular

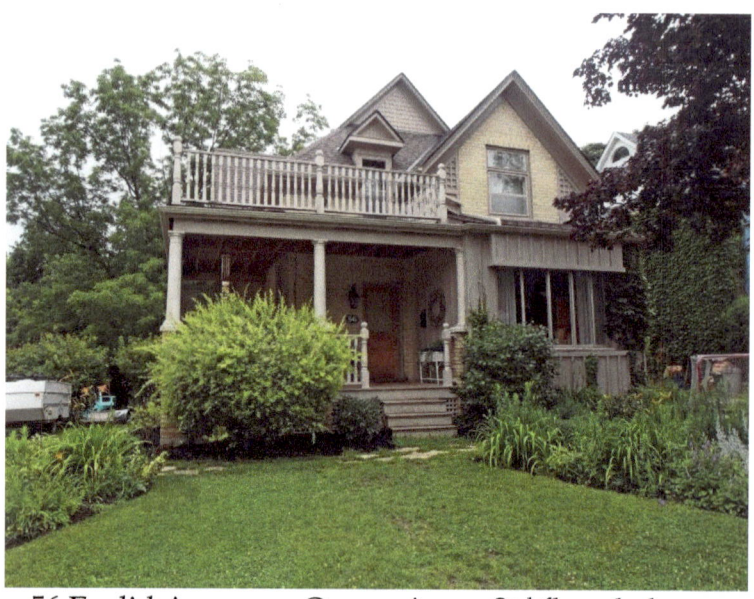

56 Euclid Avenue – Queen Anne, 2nd floor balcony

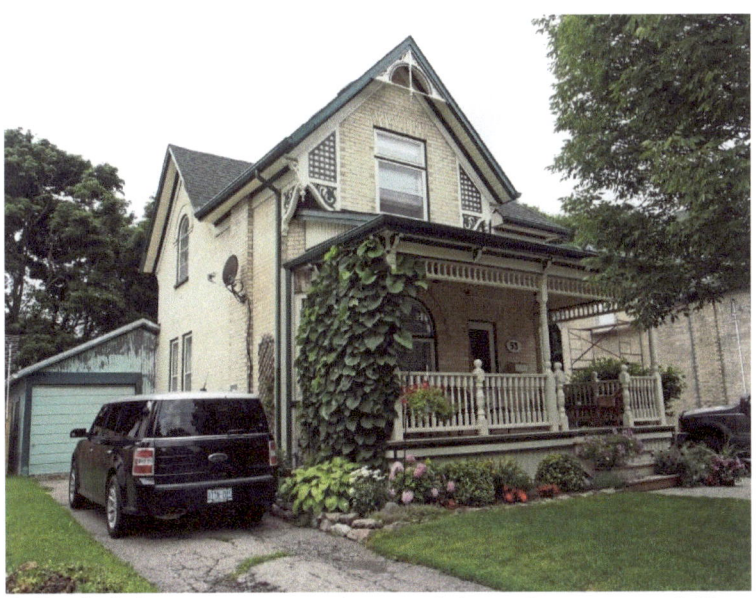

53 Euclid Avenue - turned verandah roof supports, delicate spindles; within the peak is a decorative arch with spindles; fretwork, arched window voussoirs; some round windows

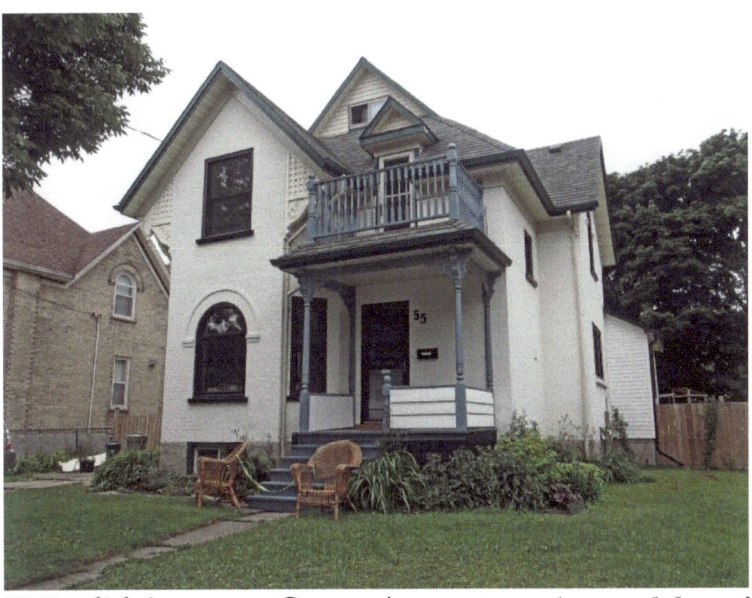

55 Euclid Avenue – Queen Anne - turned verandah roof supports, delicate spindles, intricately detailed woodwork

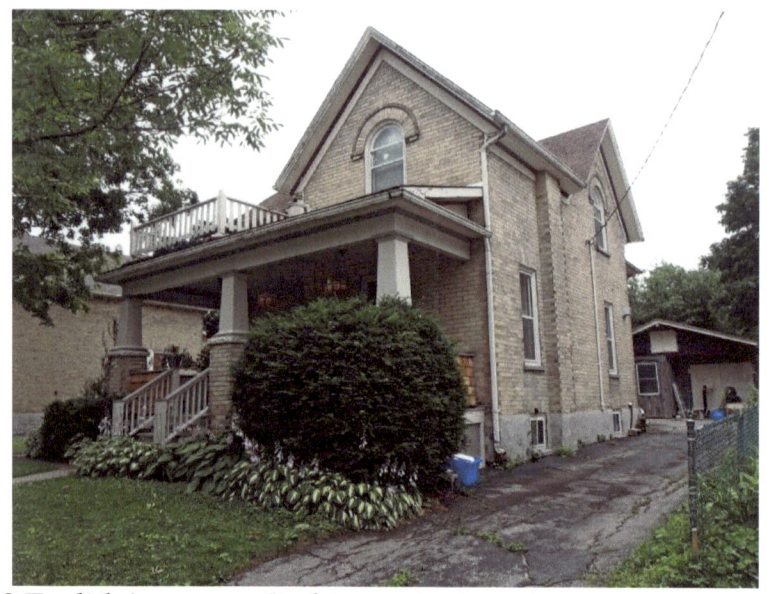

63 Euclid Avenue – Gothic - arched window voussoirs; some round windows; second floor balcony

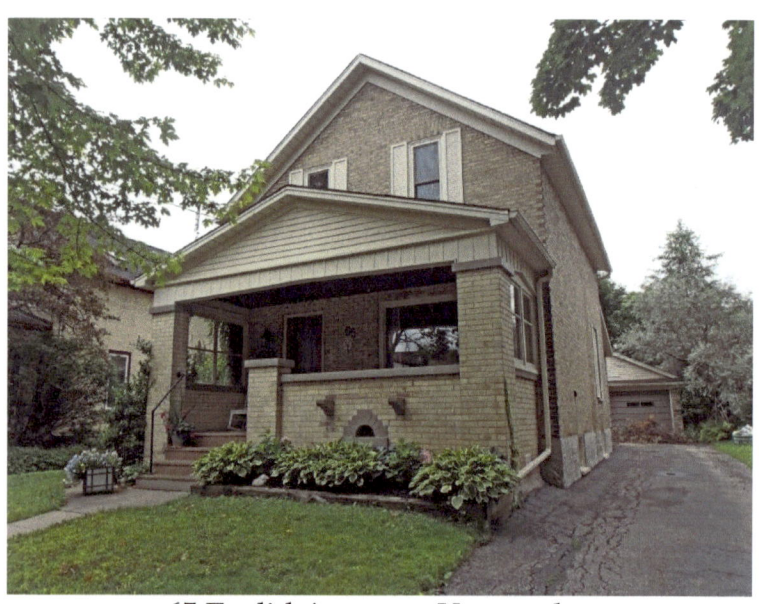

65 Euclid Avenue - Vernacular

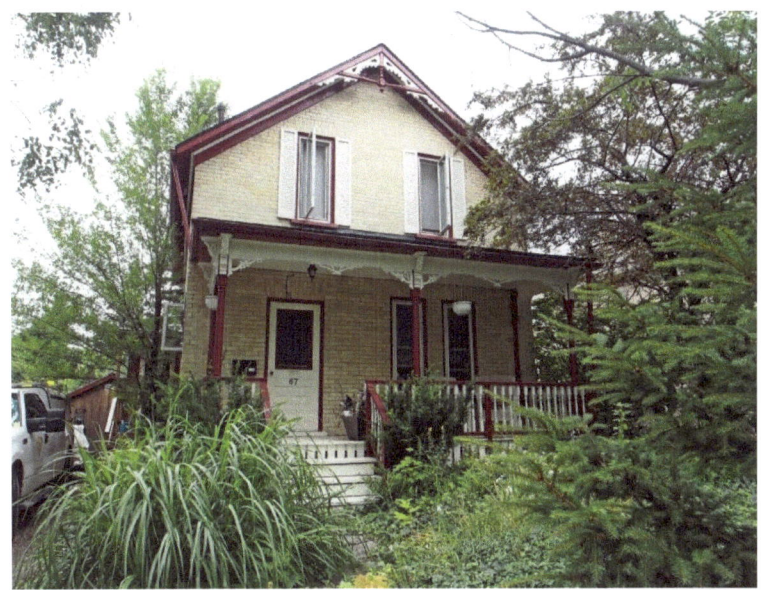

67 Euclid Avenue - turned verandah roof supports, delicate spindles, intricately detailed woodwork; within peak of gable is a decorative arch with applied scrollwork, spindles & piercing

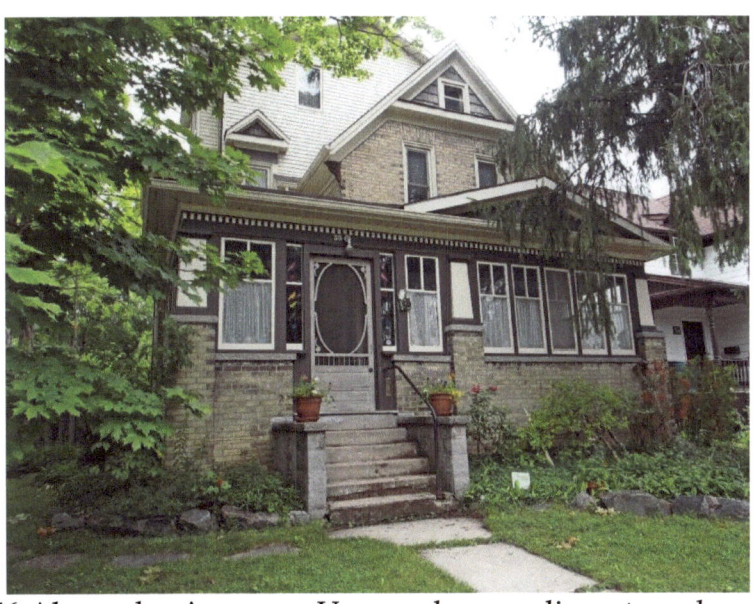

56 Alexandra Avenue – Vernacular – pediment, enclosed porch, corner cornice bracket

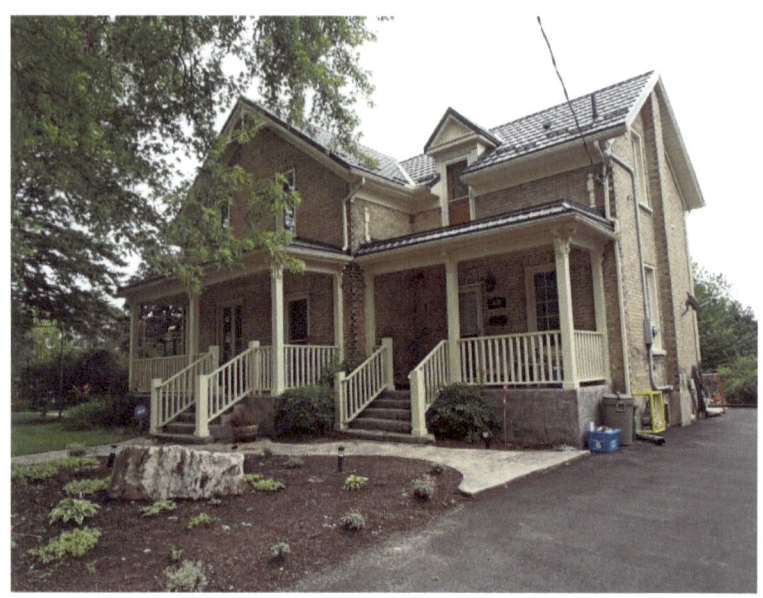

49 Alexandra Avenue – Gothic Revival - within peak of gable is a decorative arch with applied scrollwork, spindles & piercing

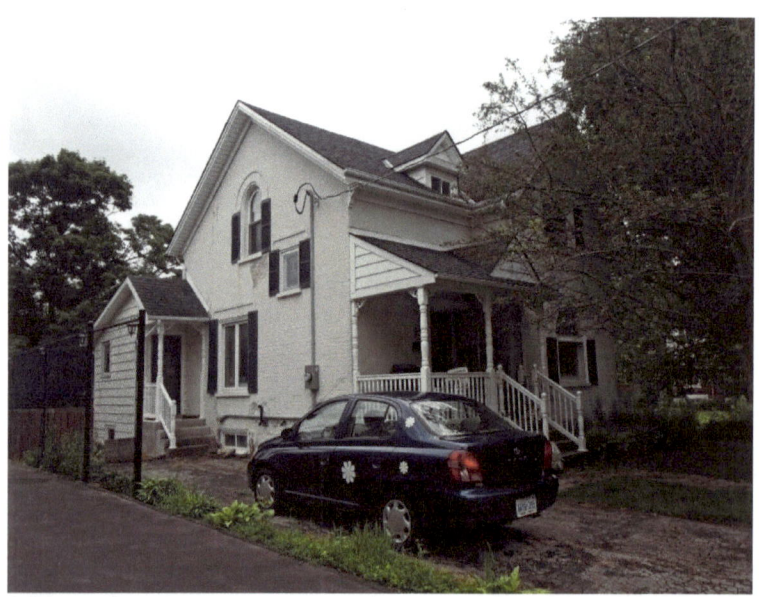

53 Alexandra Avenue – round second floor window, dormer in attic; turned verandah roof supports, delicate spindles, intricately detailed woodwork

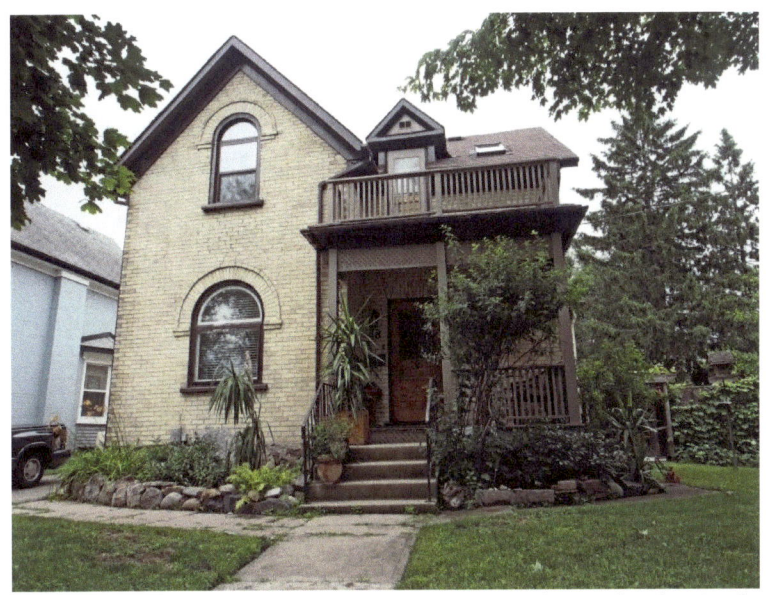

48 Alexandra Avenue – Romanesque style arched window voussoirs, 2nd floor balcony

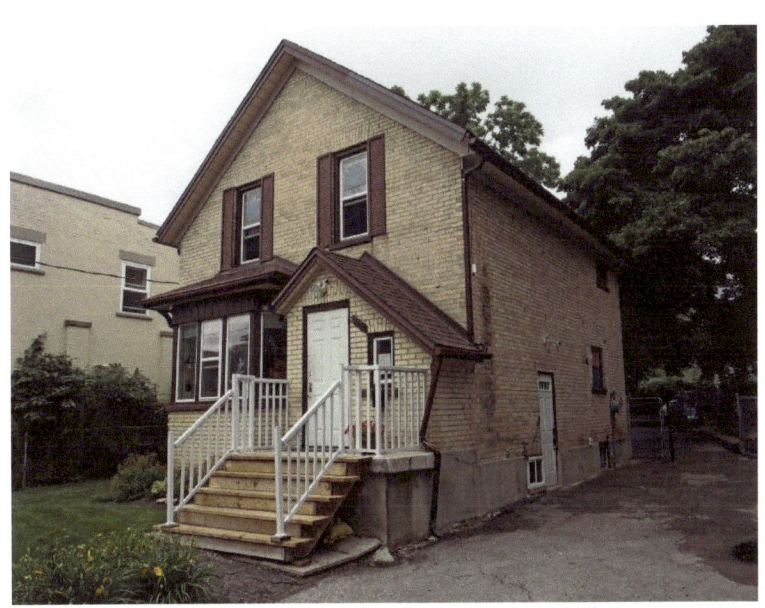

68 Alexandra Avenue – Vernacular

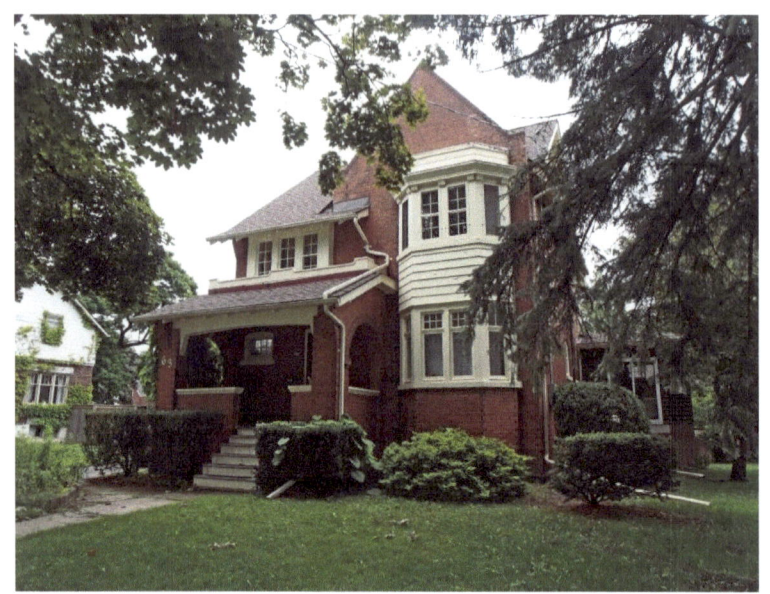

63 Alexandra Avenue - Vernacular

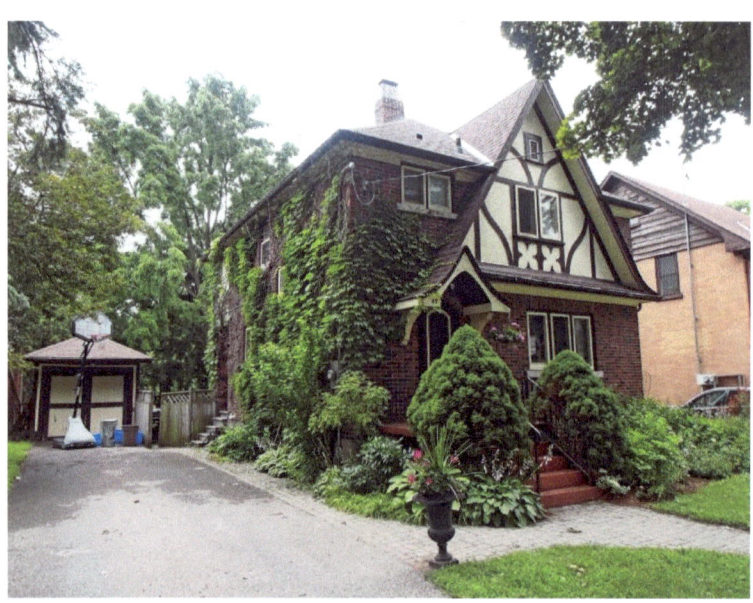

67 Alexandra Avenue – Tudor

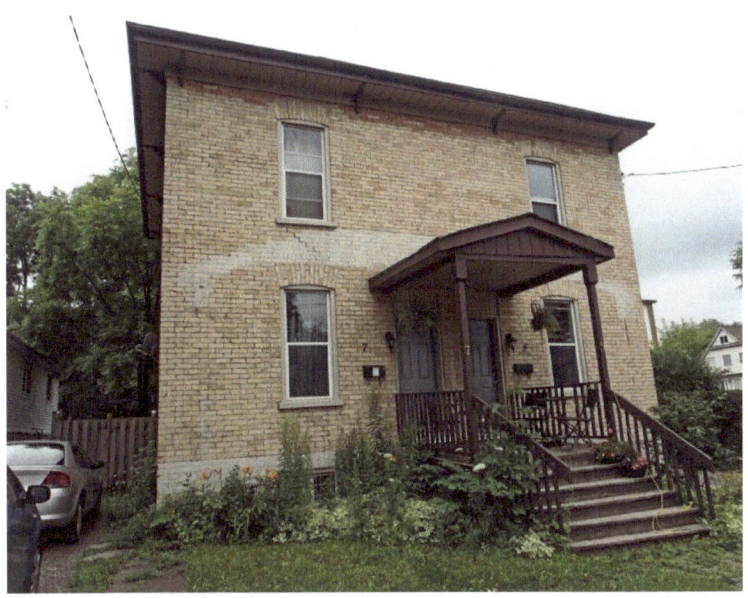

7 Menno Street – Italianate, single cornice brackets

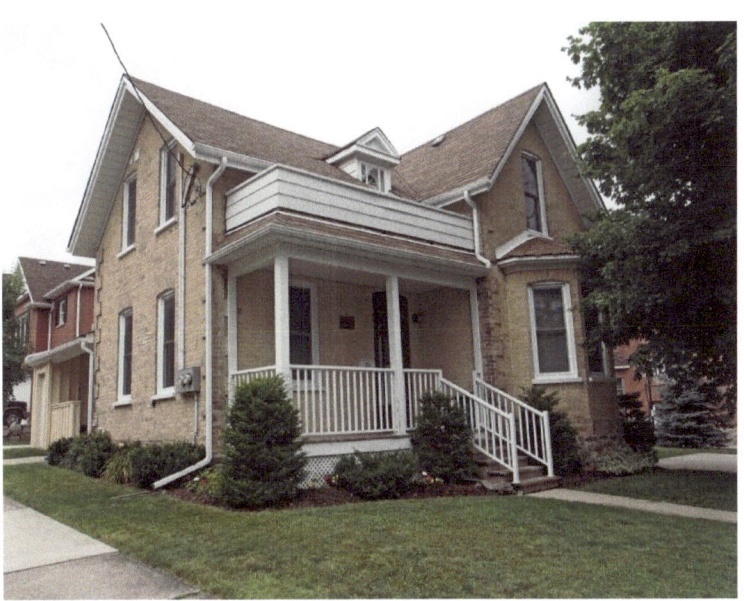

25 Menno Street – Gothic Revival, dormer in attic,
second floor balcony

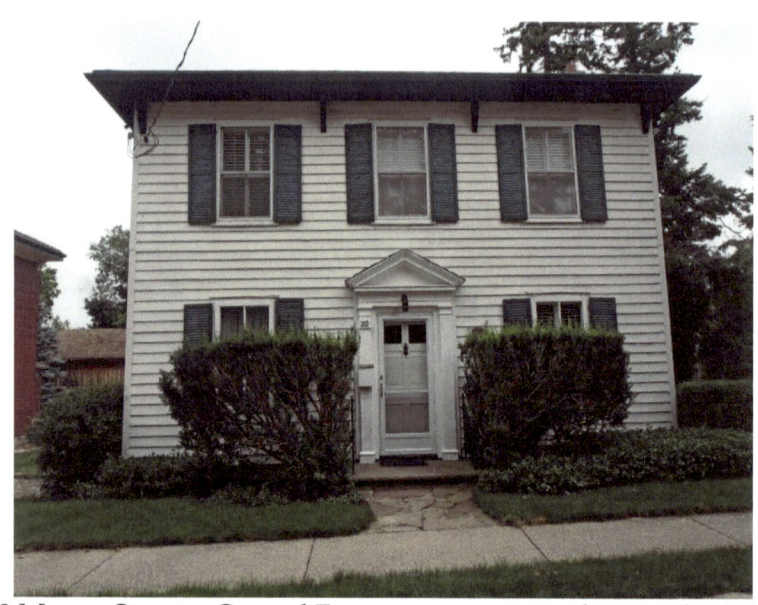

20 Menno Street – Conrad Fenner, carpenter and joiner, built his own wood frame house in 1867; he enlarged his 1½ storey home to a full 2 storeys in 1886 – Georgian style, pediment above entrance, fluted half columns, cornice brackets, granite fieldstone foundation

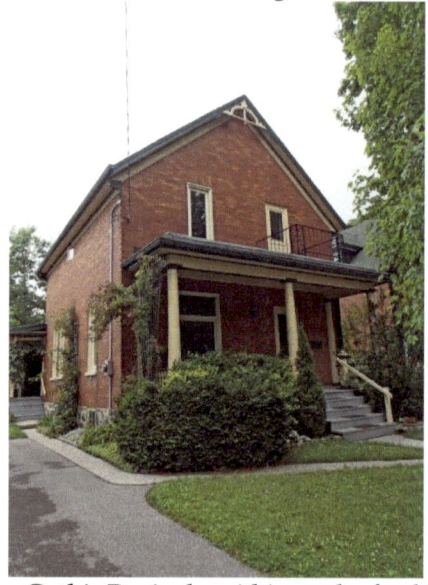

49 Menno Street – Gothic Revival - within peak of gable is a decorative arch with applied scrollwork, spindle and circular piercing

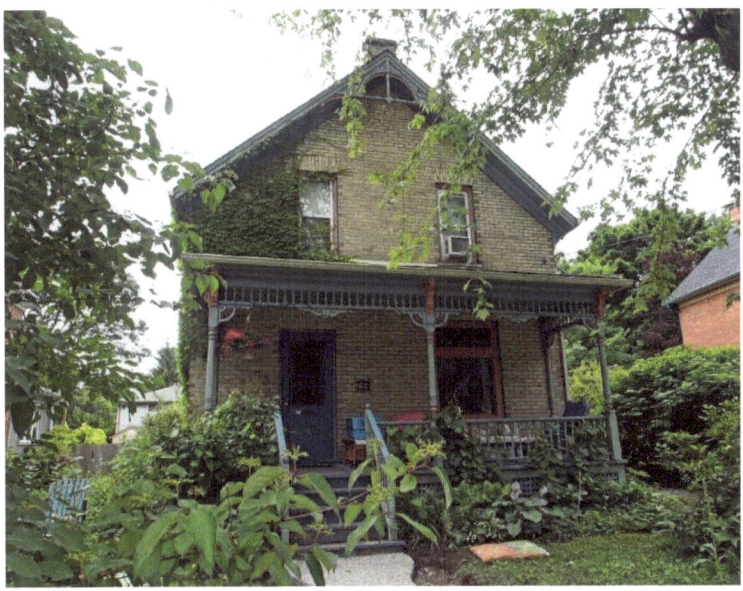

53 Menno Street – Gothic Revival - turned verandah roof supports, delicate spindles, intricately detailed woodwork, cornice brackets; within peak of gable is a decorative arch with applied scrollwork & spindle

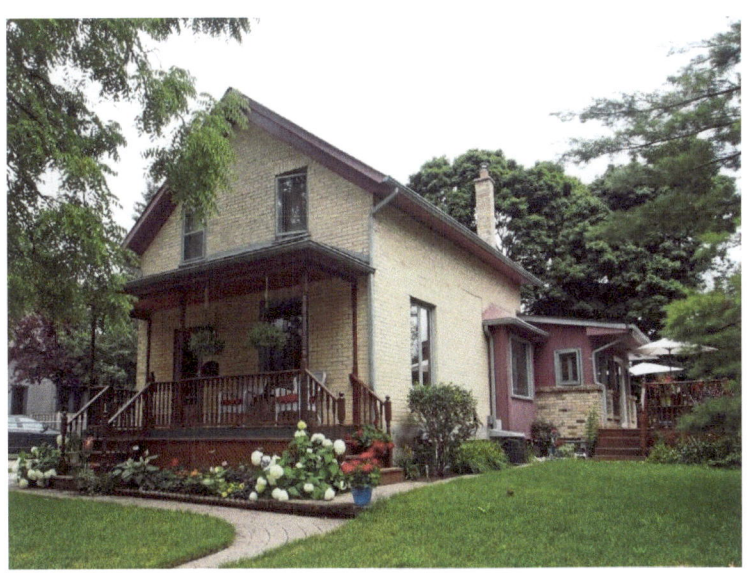

58 Menno Street – Gothic Revival

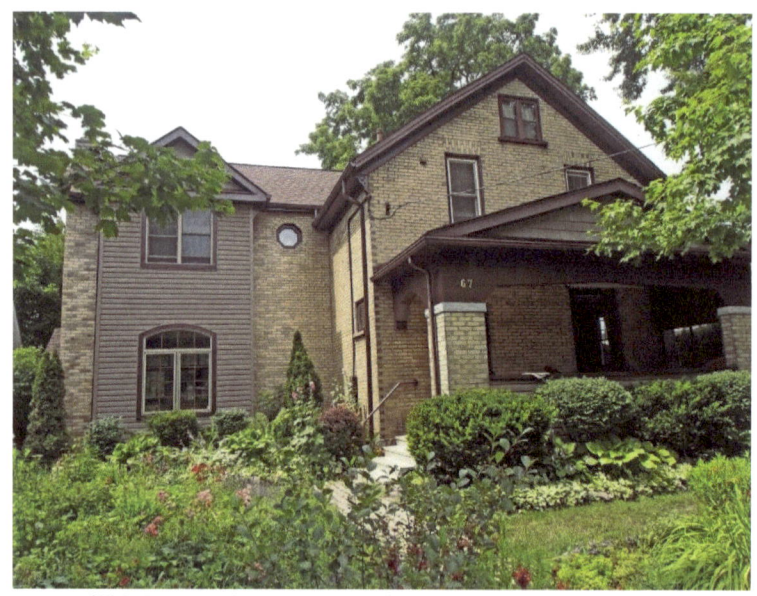

67 Menno Street – Gothic Revival, pediment

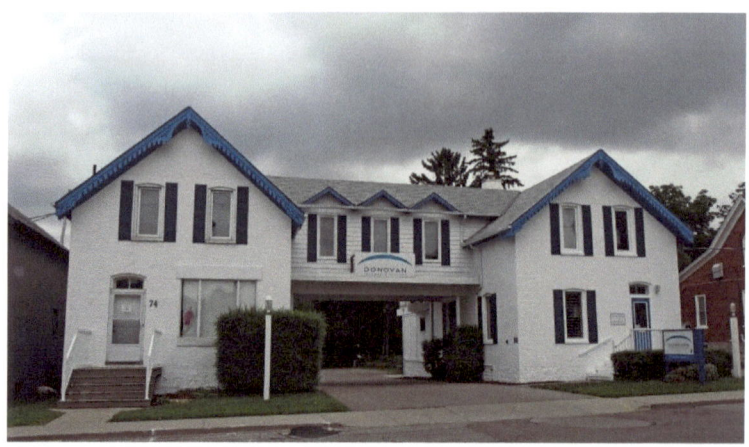

74 Regina Street North – Gothic, bargeboard trim on gables

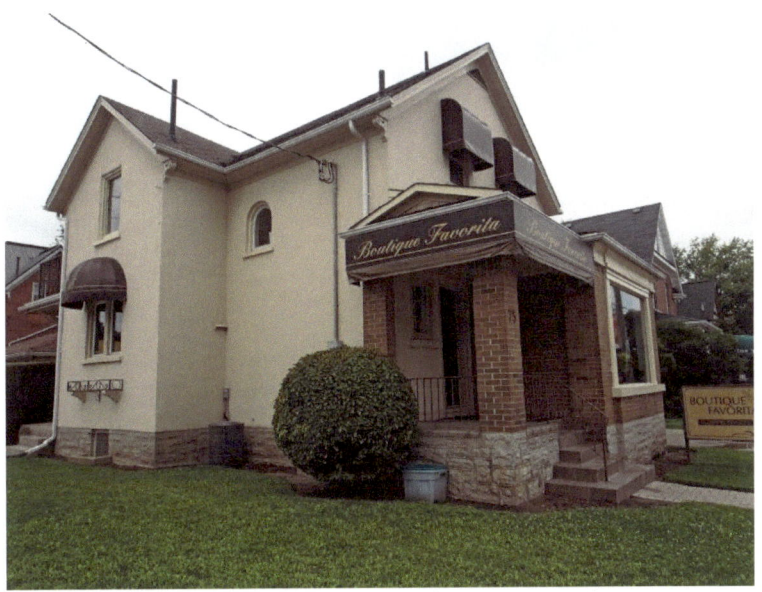

75 Regina Street North - Vernacular

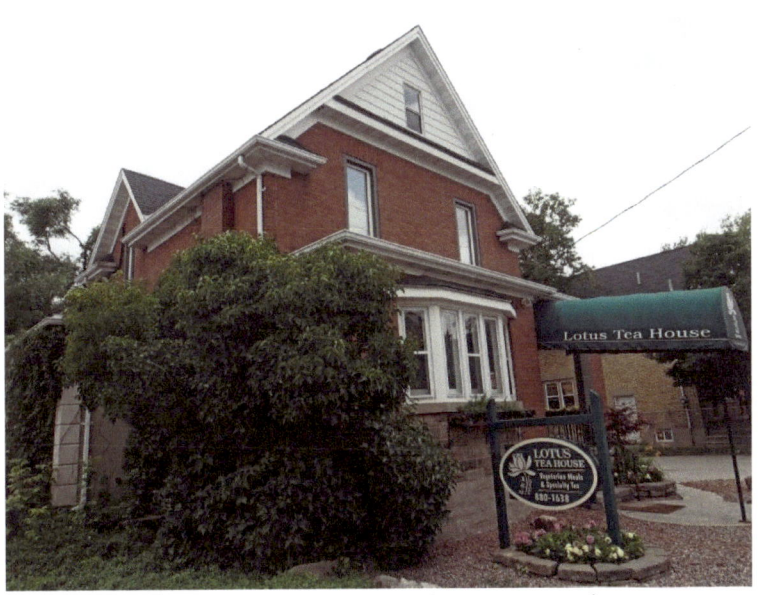

79 Regina Street North - Vernacular

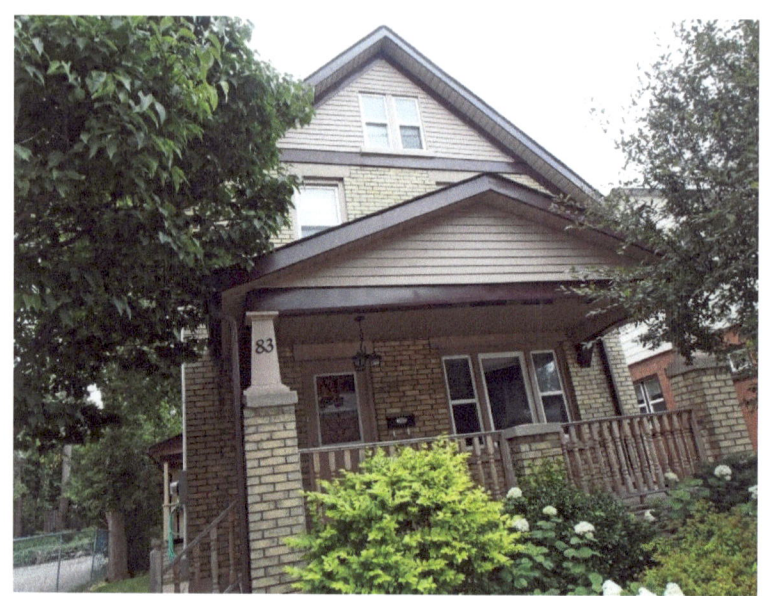

83 Regina Street North - Vernacular

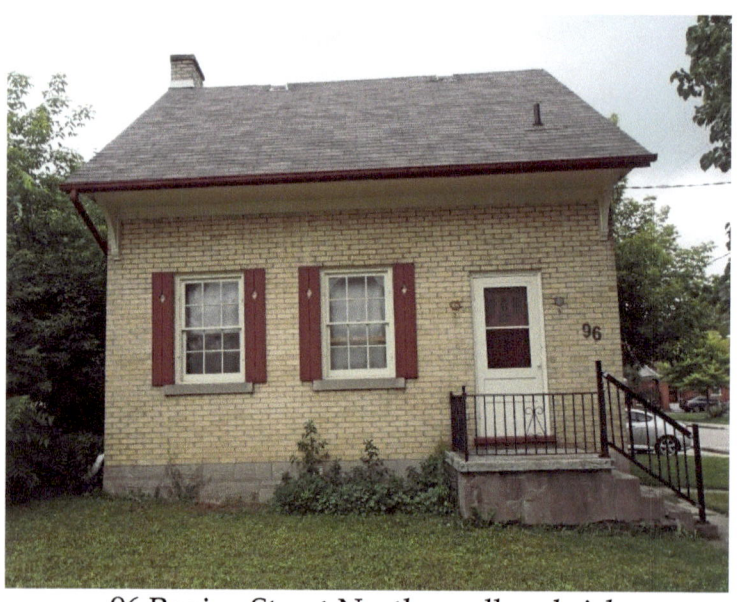

96 Regina Street North – yellow brick

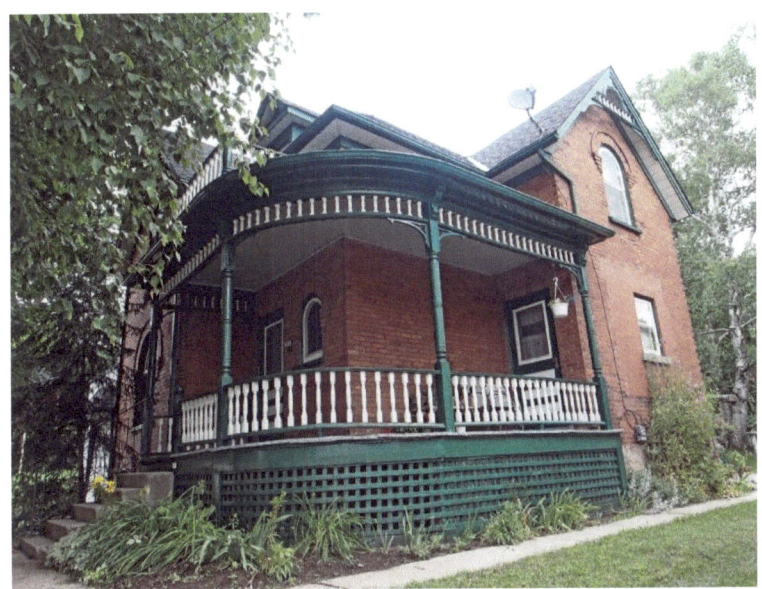

104 Regina Street North – Queen Anne - turned verandah roof supports, delicate spindles, intricately detailed woodwork; within peak of gable is a decorative arch with applied scrollwork

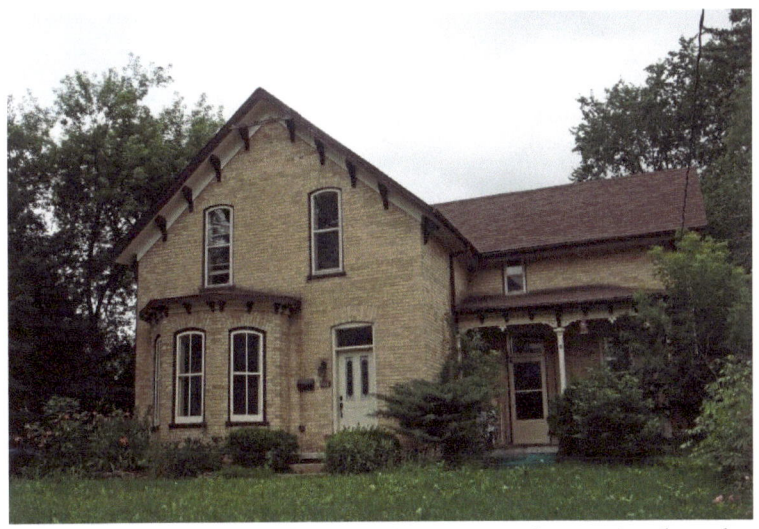

106 Regina Street North – Gothic Revival, cornice brackets, bay window with brackets

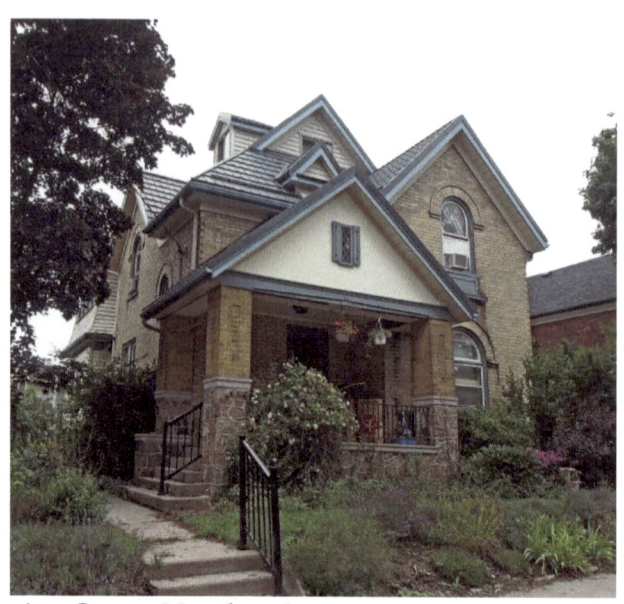

107 Regina Street North – Queen Anne Vernacular, round window voussoirs

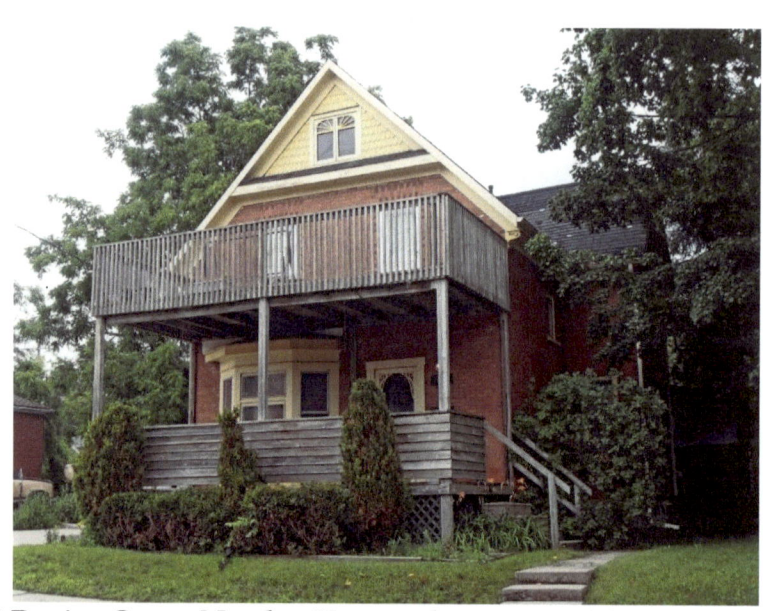

110 Regina Street North – Vernacular – second floor full-width verandah, ground floor bay window

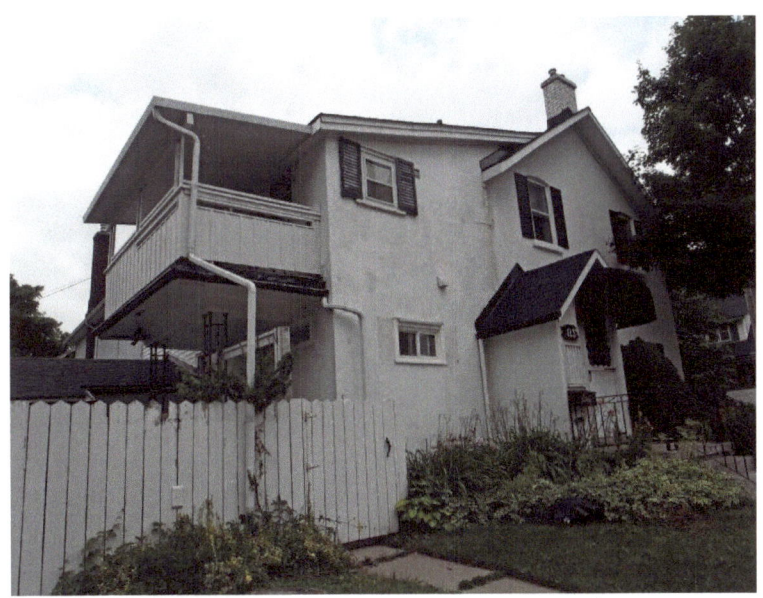

113 Regina Street North – Vernacular –
2nd floor balcony on side

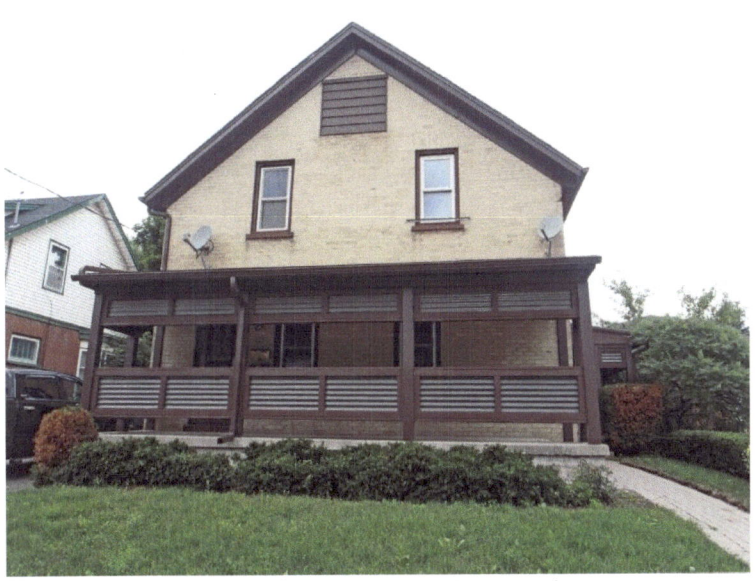

16 Noecker Street - Vernacular

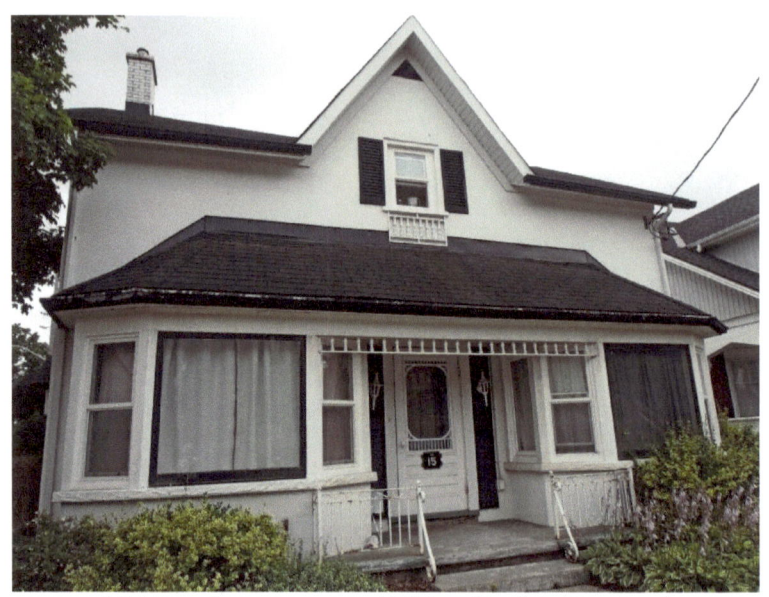

15 Noecker Street – 1879 – Gothic Revival

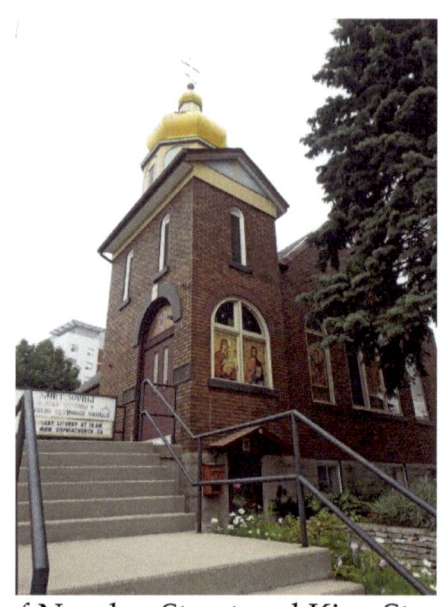

Corner of Noecker Street and King Street North
– Saint Sophia Greek Orthodox Church

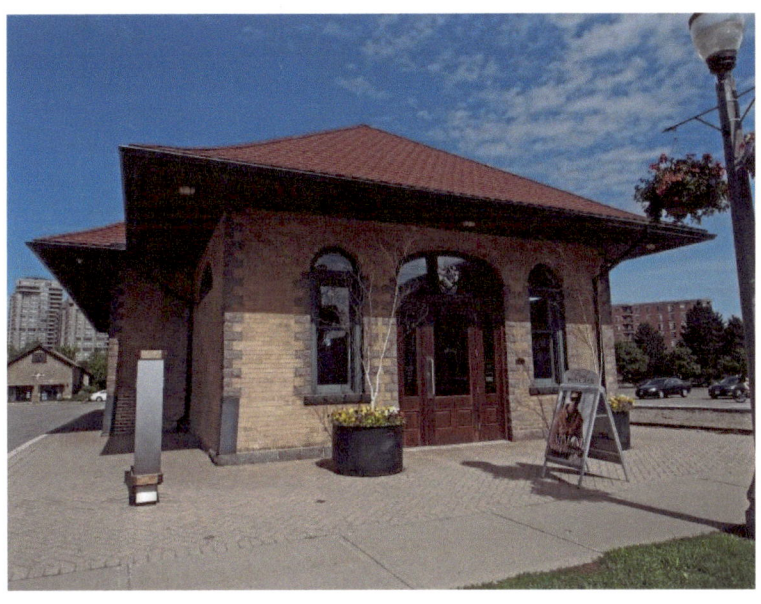

Regina Street South at Erb Street – restored old train station

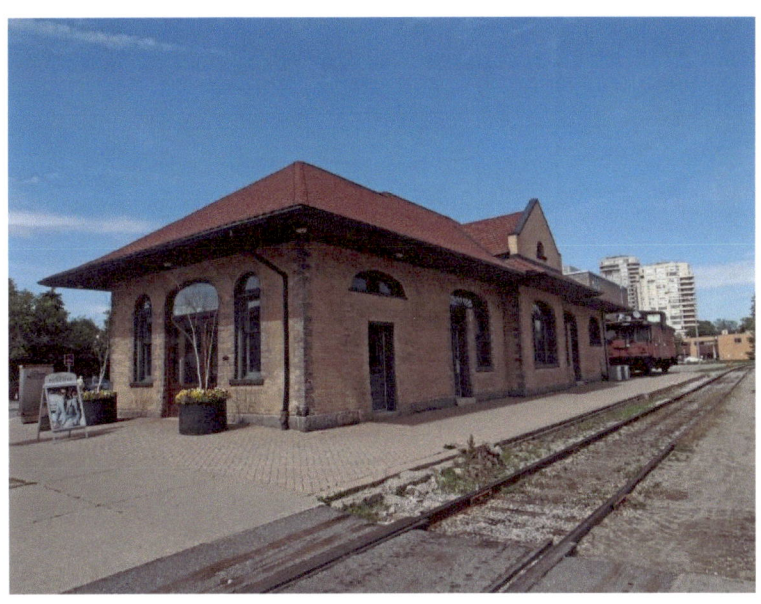

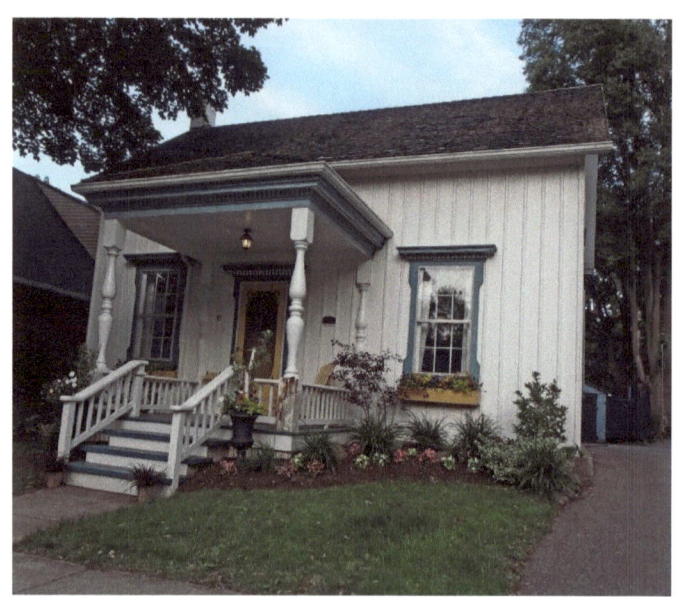

81 Norman Street - 1½ storey frame house – Vernacular board and batten; both the six-over-six paned windows and the front entrance feature eared trim with the architraves above those openings having dentils

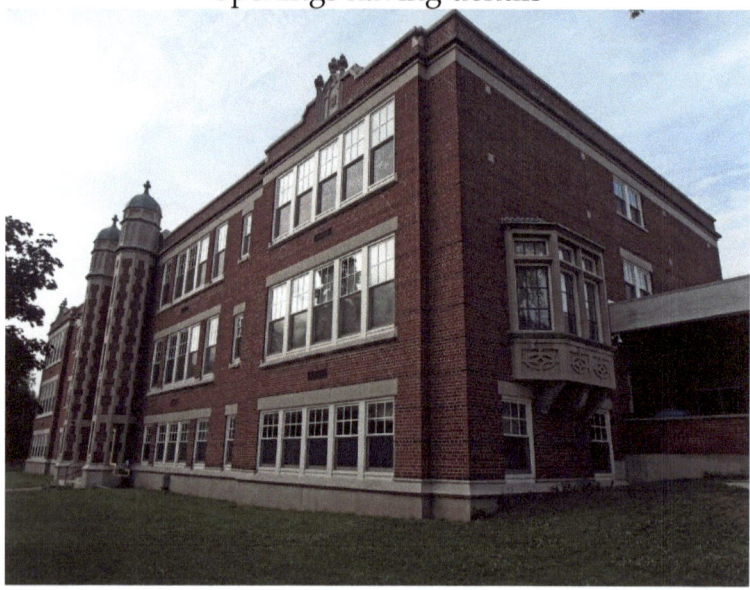

Elizabeth Ziegler School - 3 storey red brick and grey stone Gothic Revival style – large single-storey stone oriel window on end

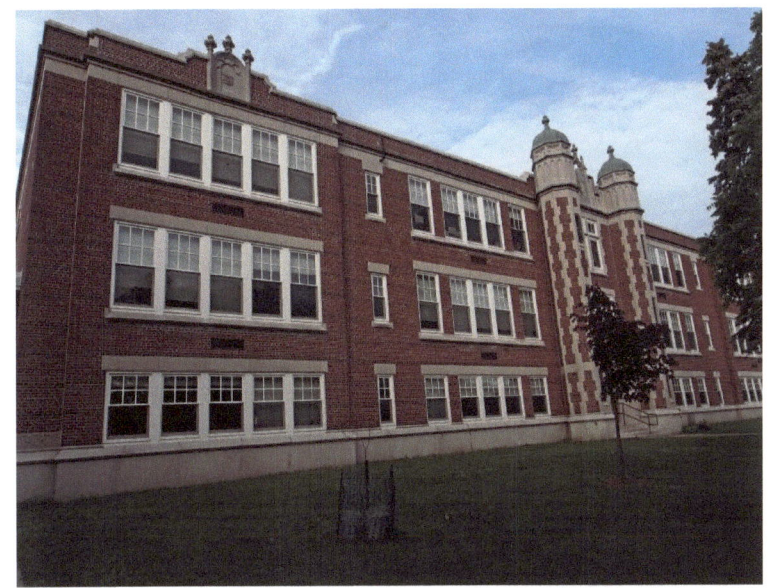

90 Moore Avenue South – 1931 - Elizabeth Ziegler Public School named in honour of a local teacher who had completed fifty-five years of service in 1930

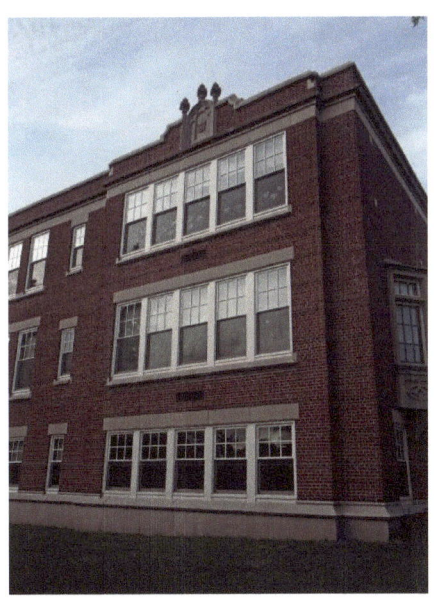

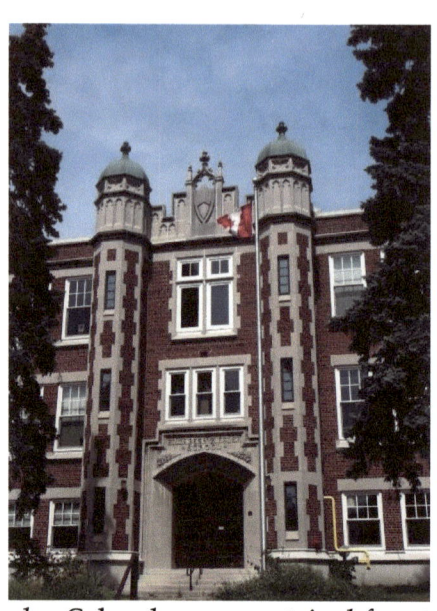

Elizabeth Ziegler School - symmetrical front façade, main entrance deeply inset, framed in stone; pair of tall brick-and-stone turrets of pseudo-Tudor design with graceful octagonal copper-sheathed domes; at their upper level they frame a highly ornate stone pediment bearing finials in the form of *fleurs de lis*. The finials are echoed twice, in a slightly smaller size, above the parapet at each end of the front façade.

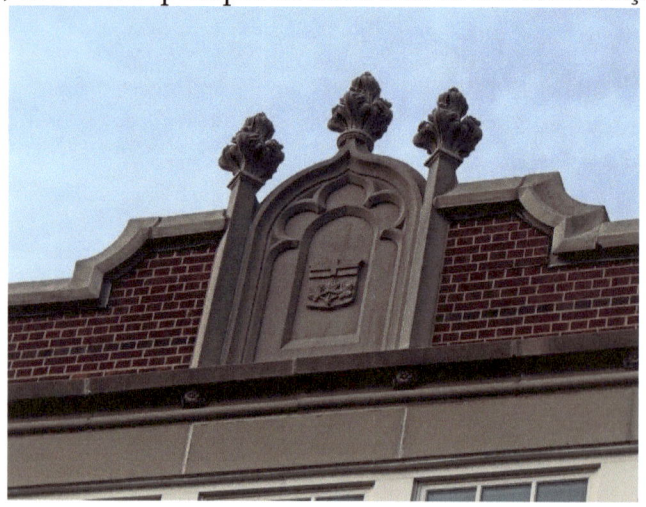

Breslau

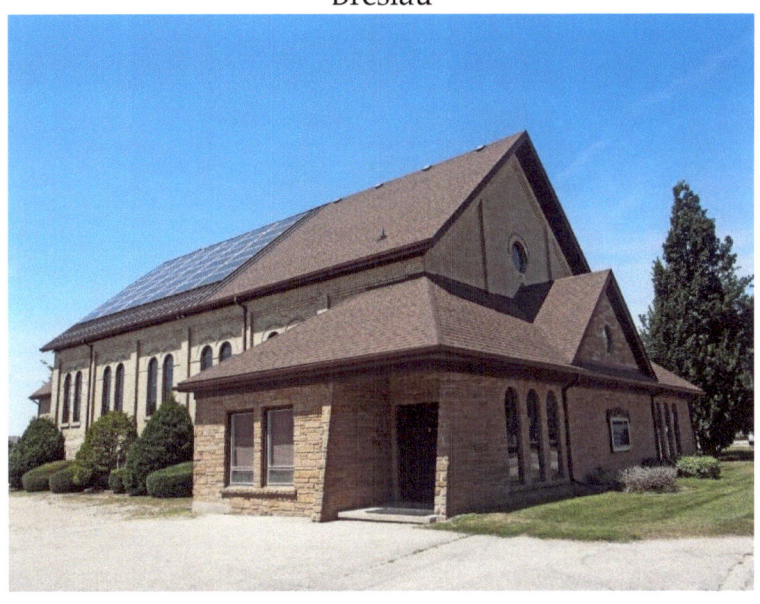

226 Woolwich Street - Breslau Mennonite Church

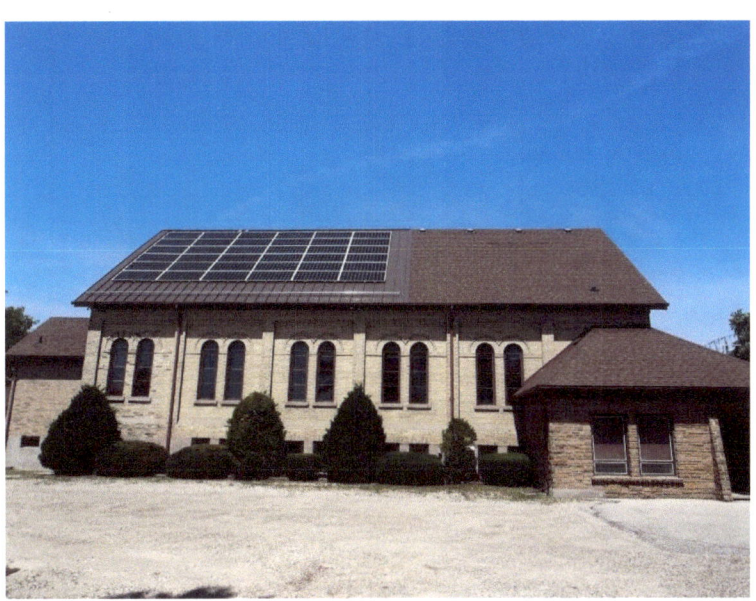

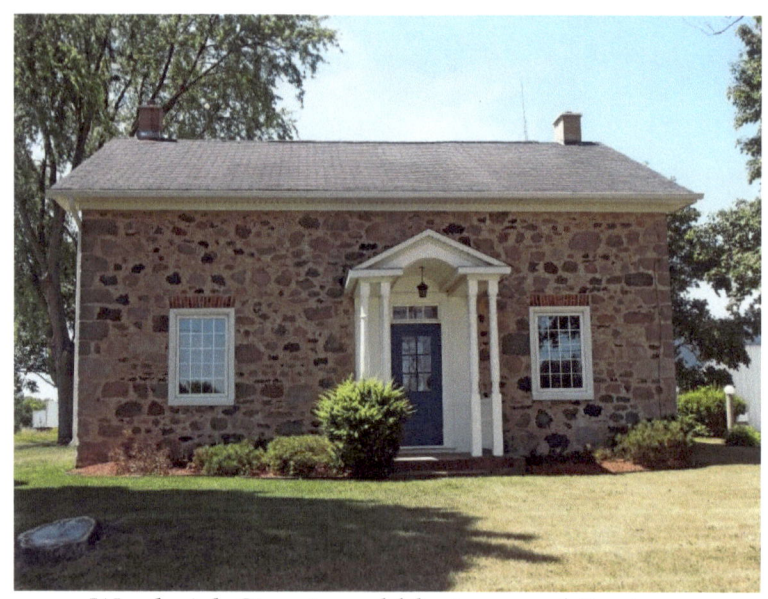

Woolwich Street – cobblestone architecture

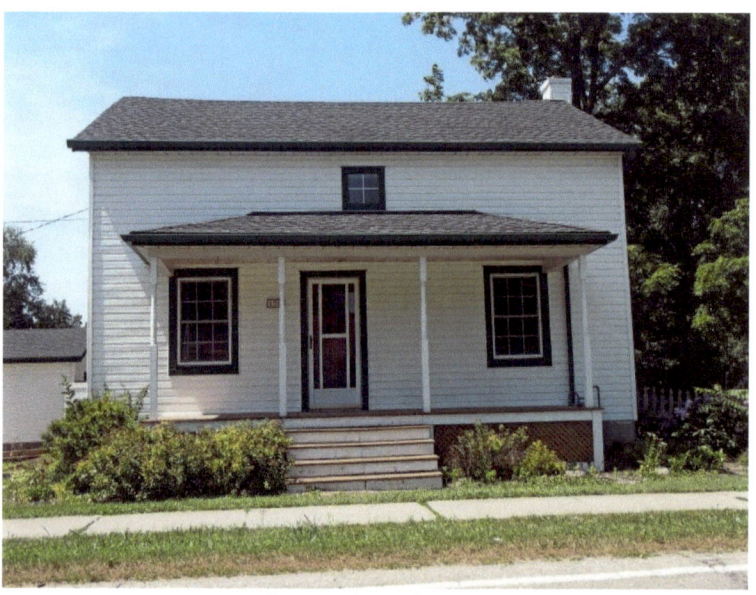

150 Woolwich Street

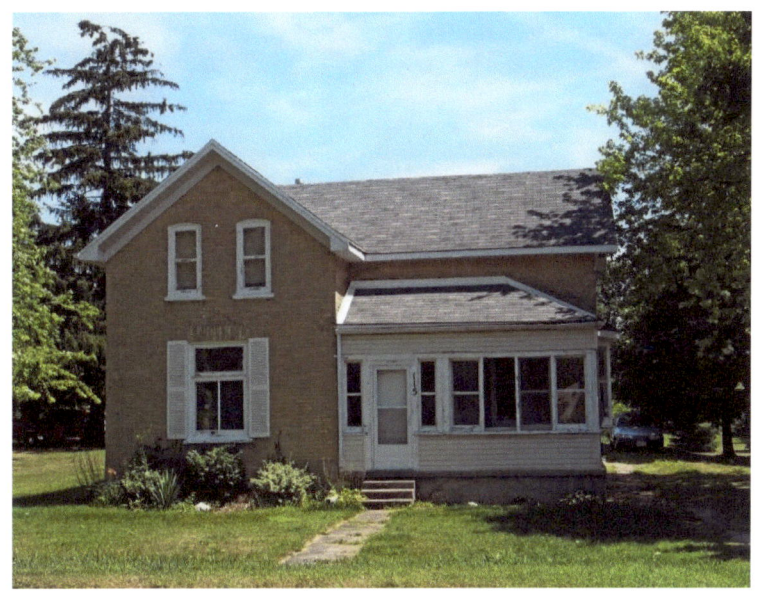

115 Woolwich Street – Gothic Revival

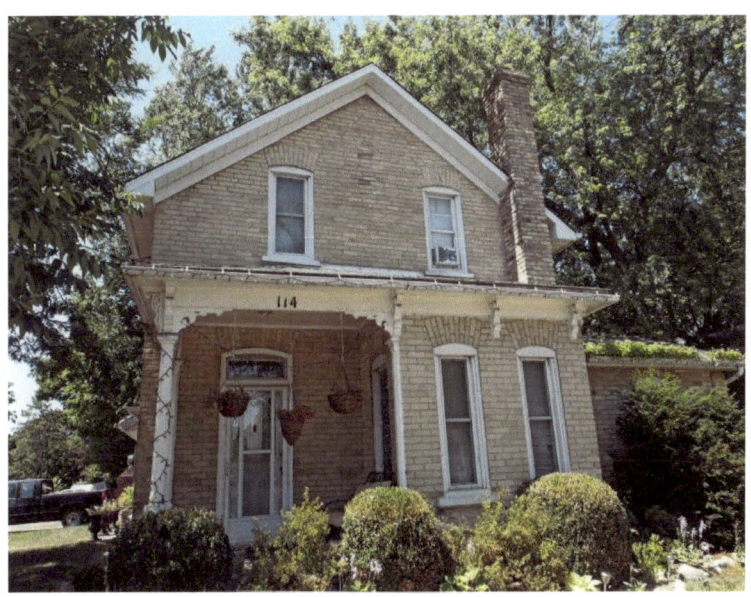

114 Woolwich Street – Gothic Revival

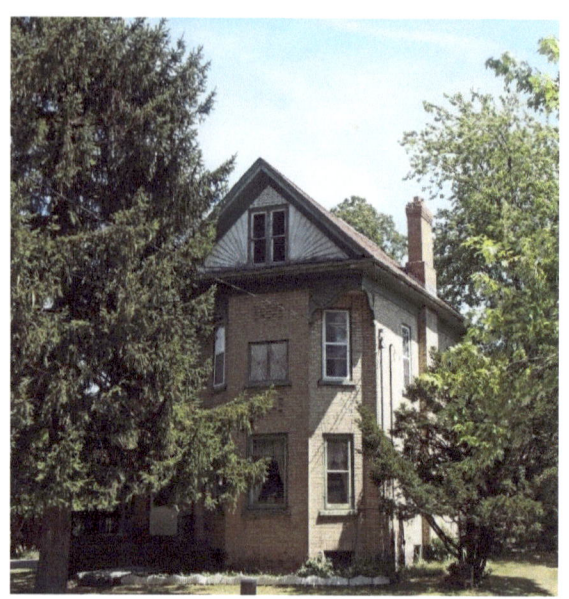

Woolwich Street – Edwardian, fretwork

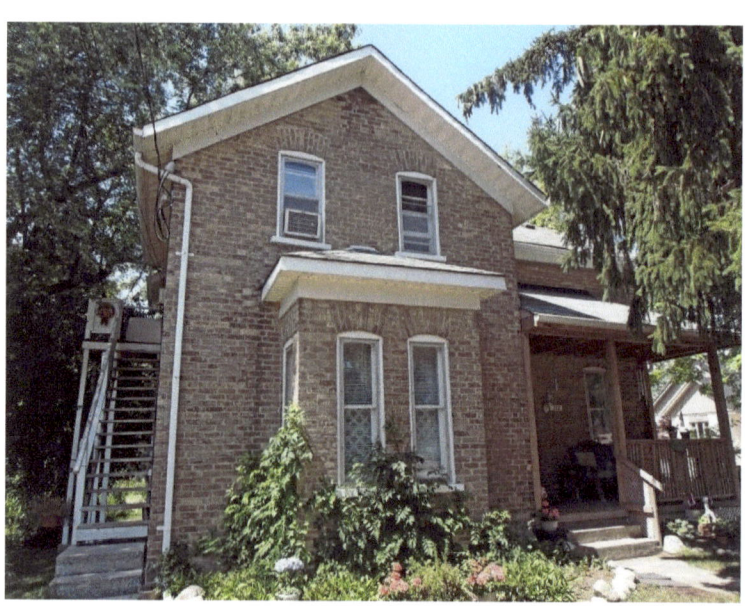

110 Woolwich Street – Gothic Revival,
rectangular bay window

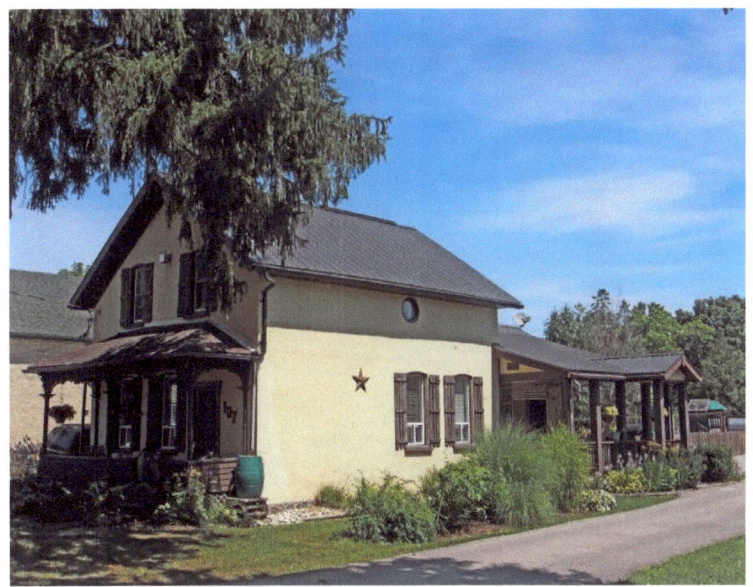

107 Woolwich Street – Gothic Revival

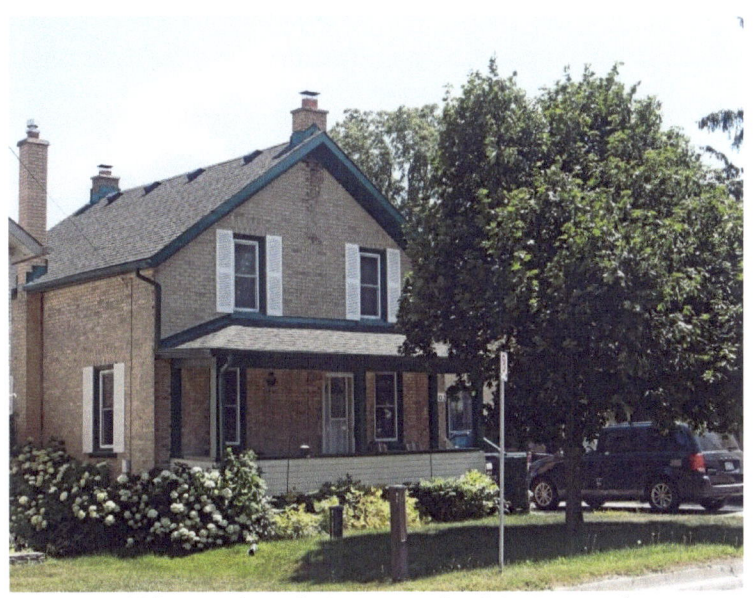

103 Woolwich Street – Gothic Revival

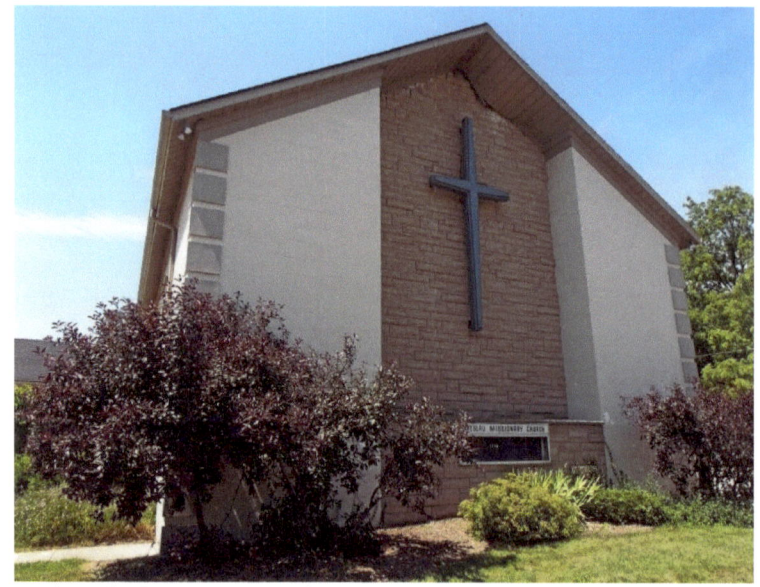

Woolwich Street – Breslau Evangelical Missionary Church

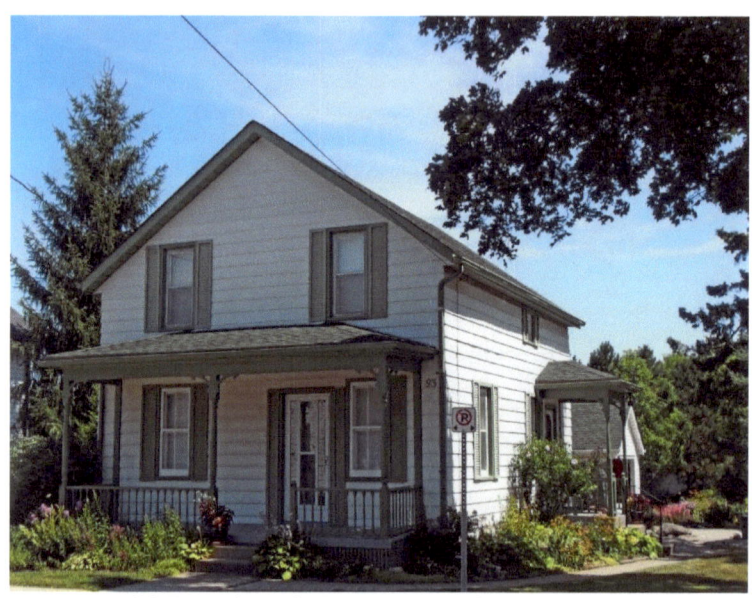

93 Woolwich Street – Gothic Revival

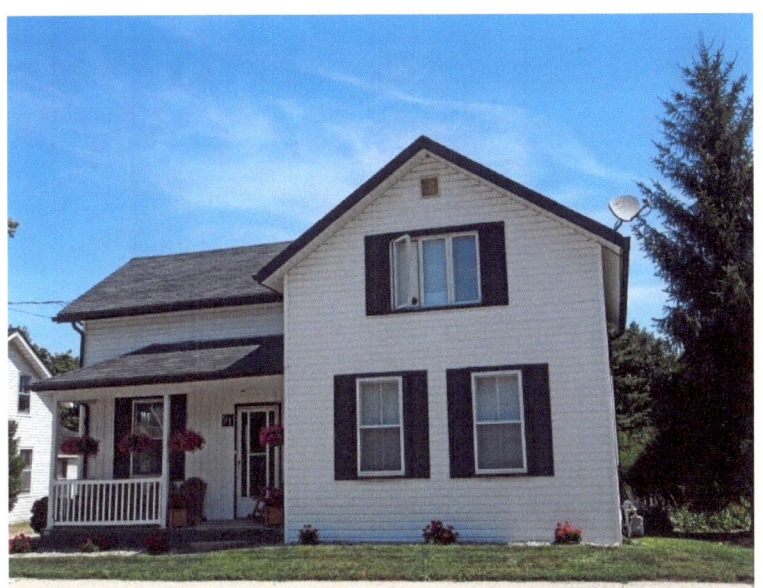

91 Woolwich Street – Gothic Revival

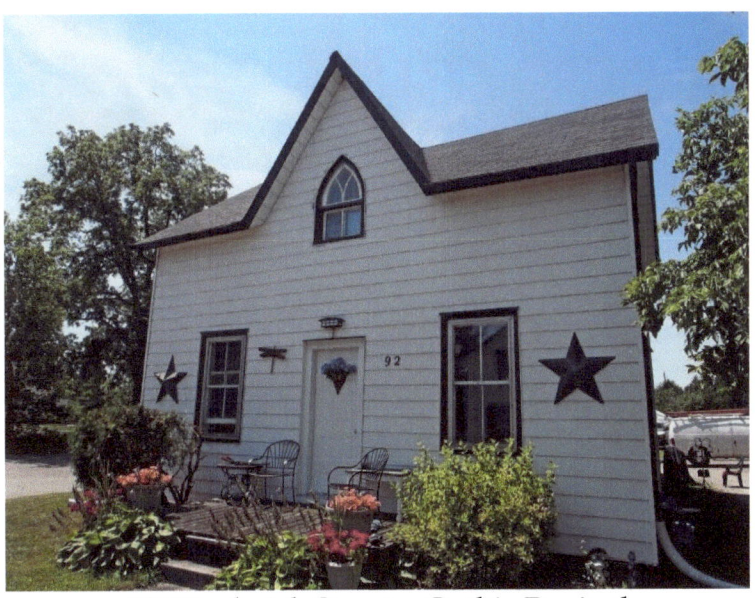

92 Woolwich Street – Gothic Revival

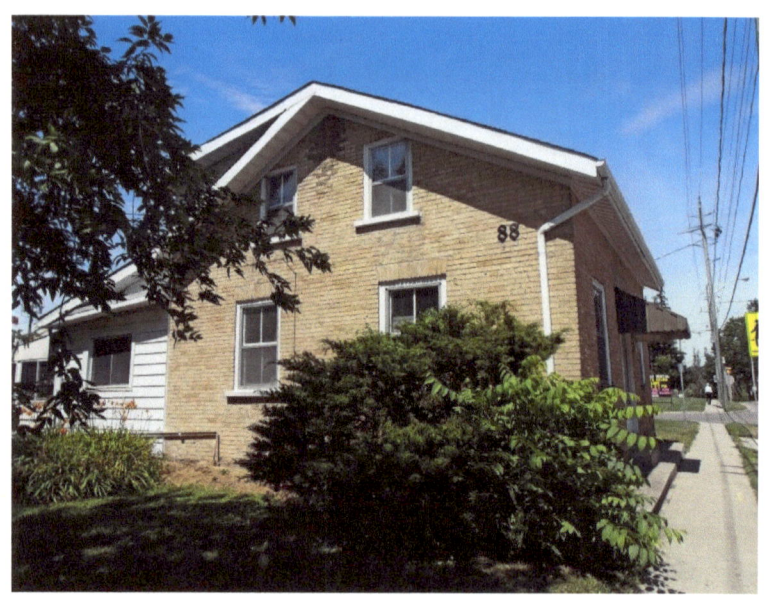

88 Woolwich Street - Vernacular

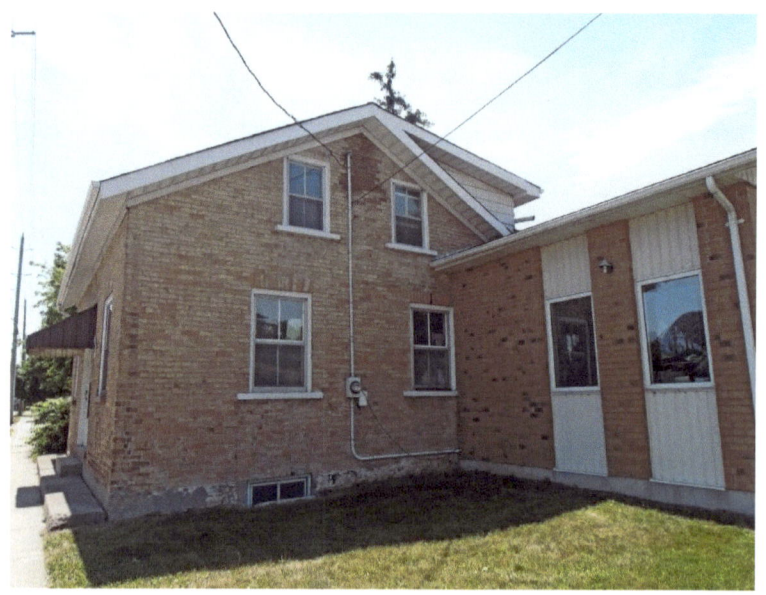

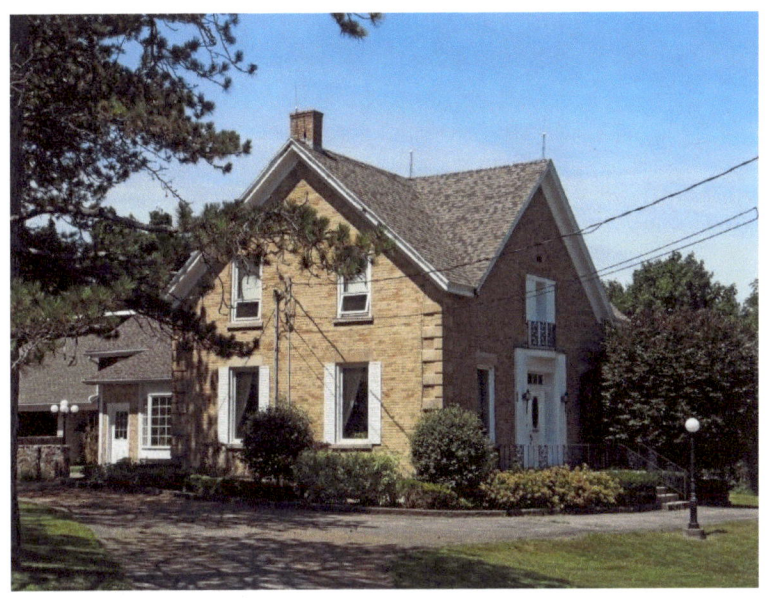

68 Woolwich Street – Gothic Revival, corner quoins

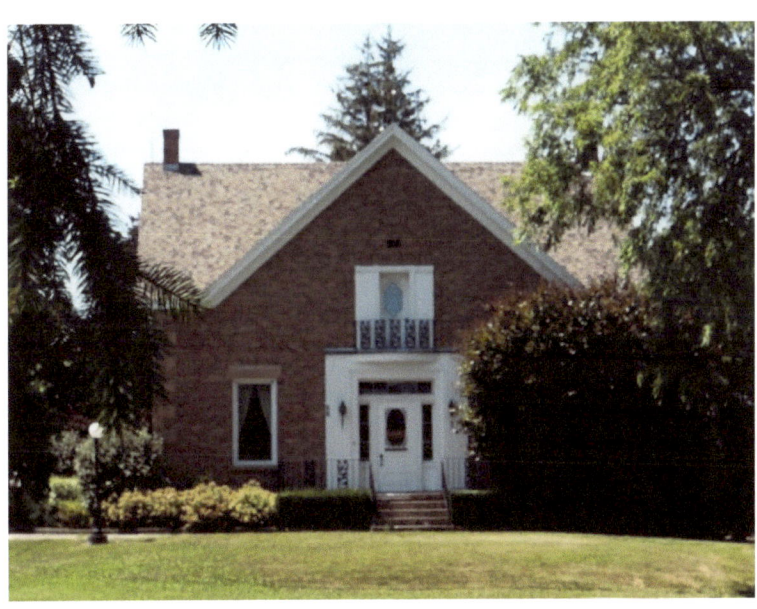

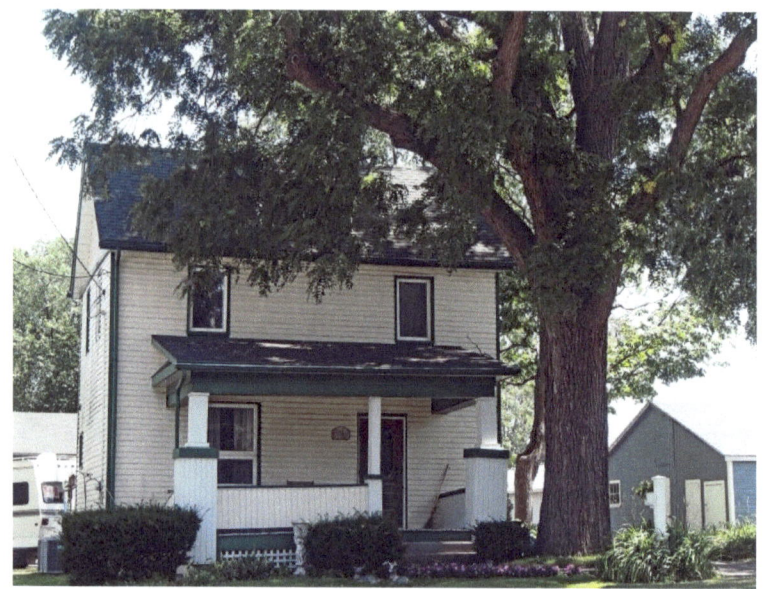

71 Woolwich Street – Gothic Revival

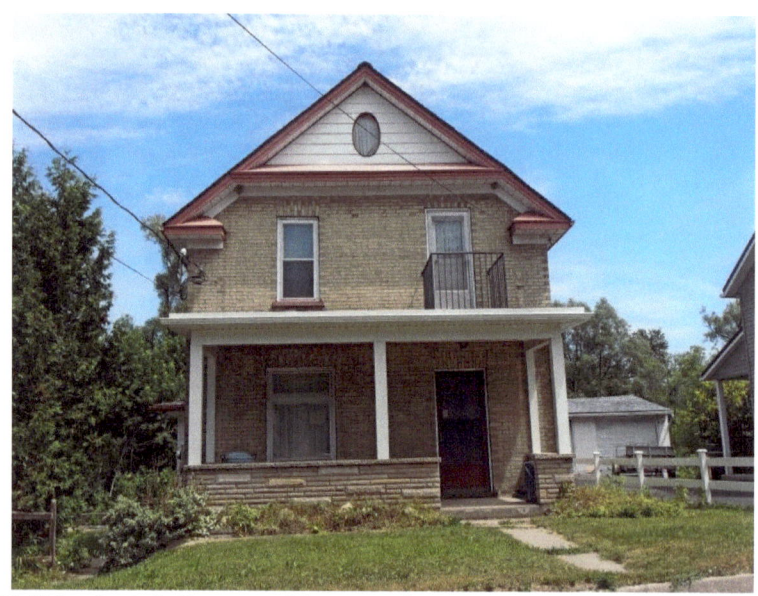

31 Woolwich Street – Vernacular, cornice return on gable

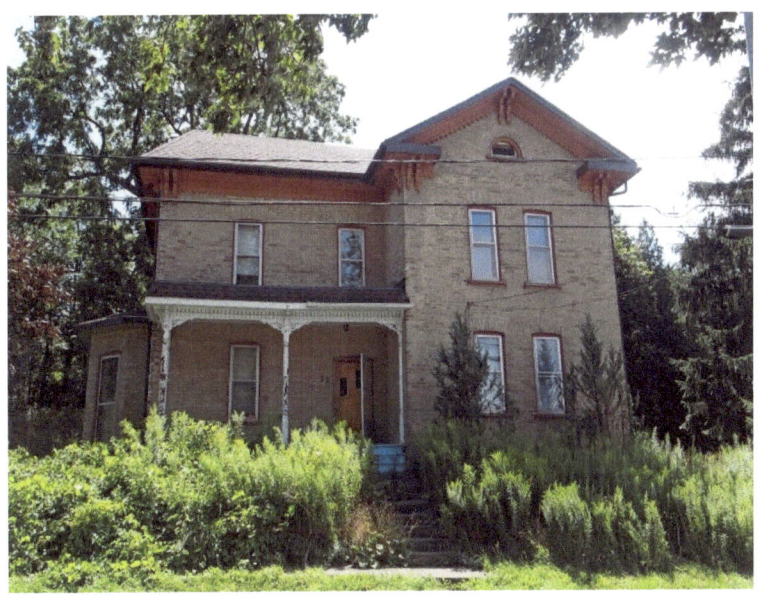

33 Scheifele Place – Italianate with 2½ storey tower-like bay, cornice brackets, turned verandah roof supports with delicate spindles

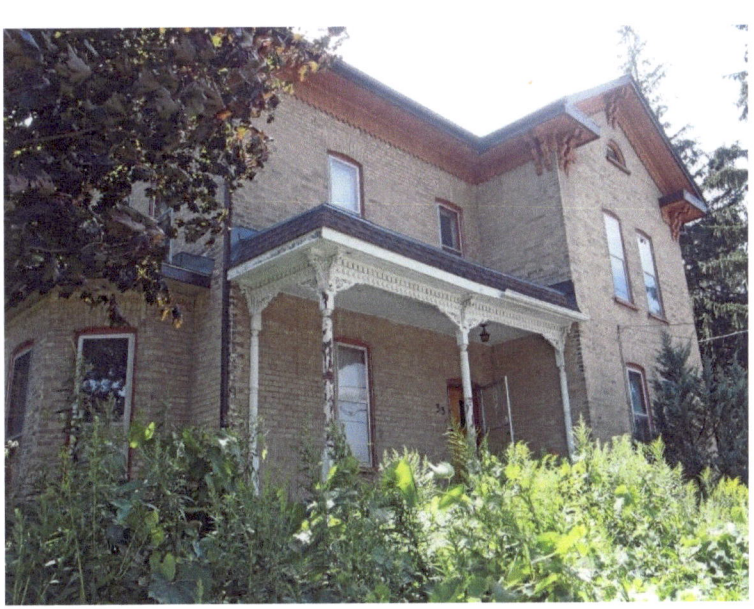

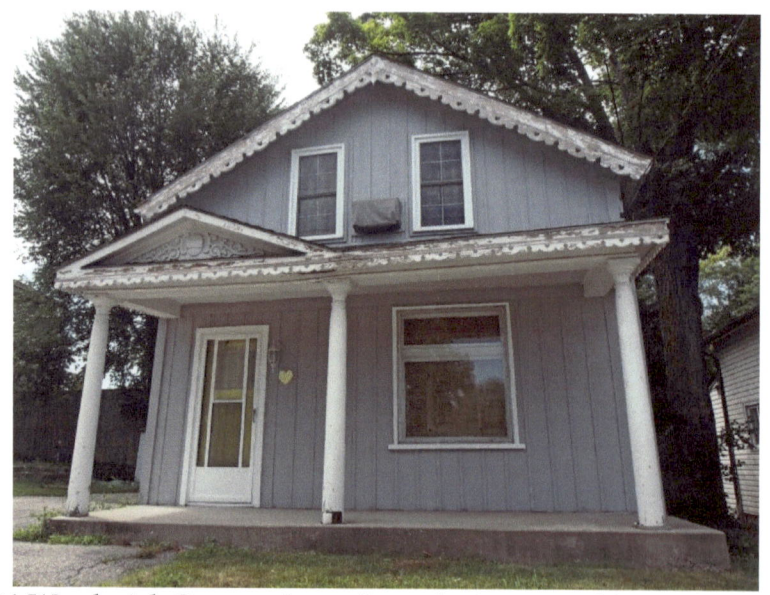

34 Woolwich Street – bargeboard trim on gable, pediment

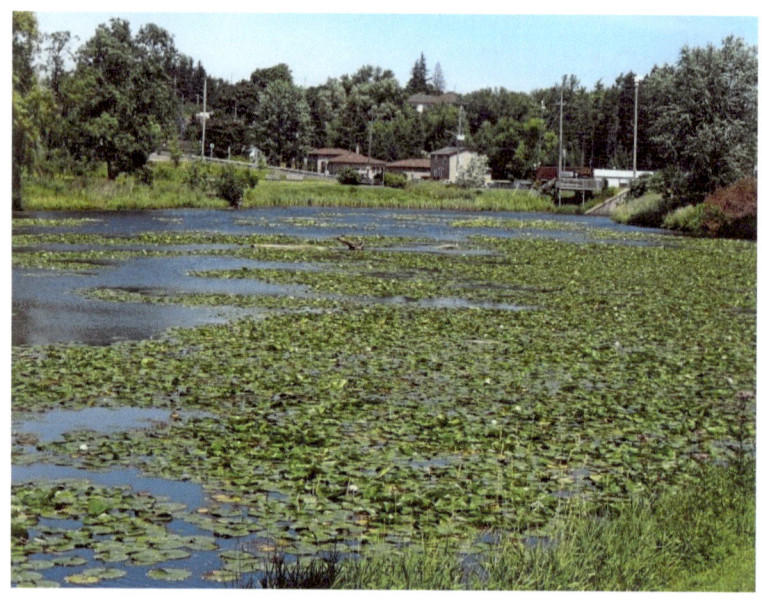

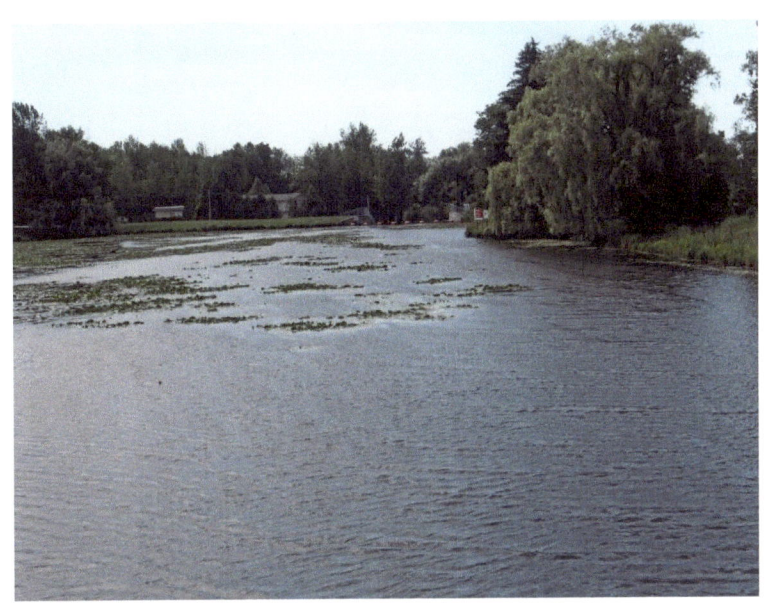

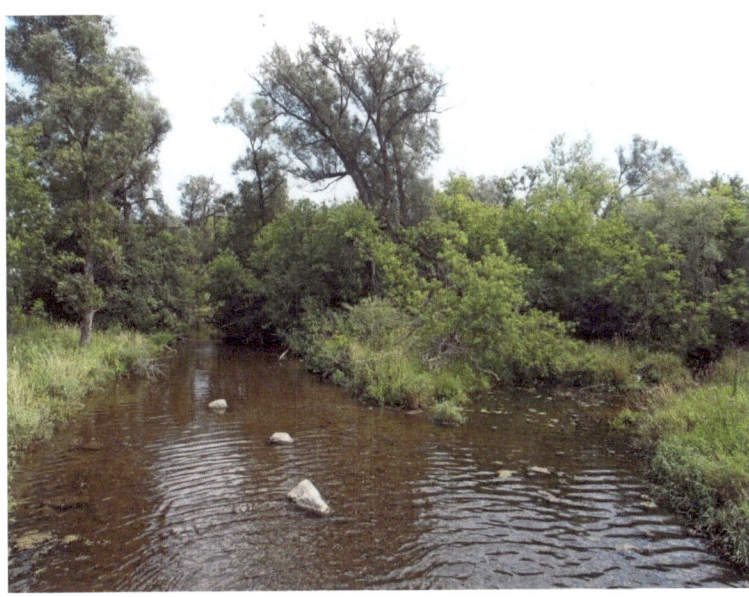

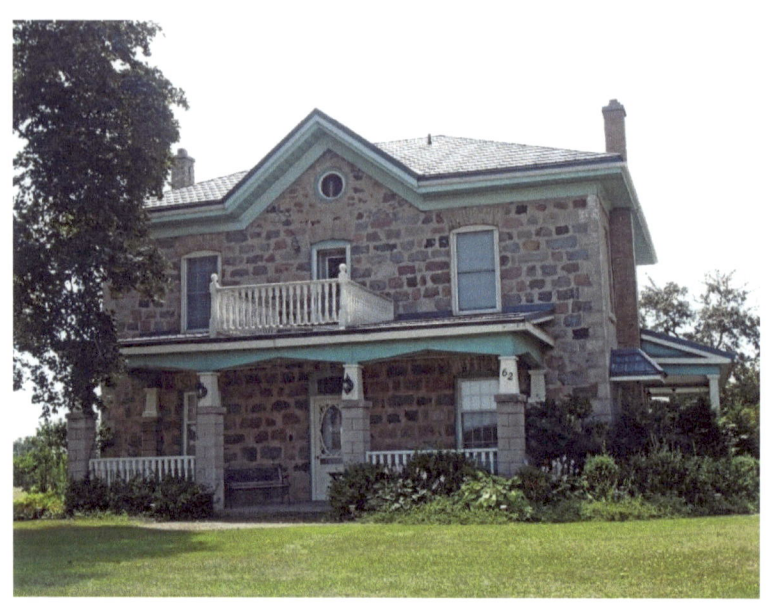

62 County Road 17 (Woolwich Street) -
Cobblestone architecture in Gothic Revival style,
second floor balcony, round attic window

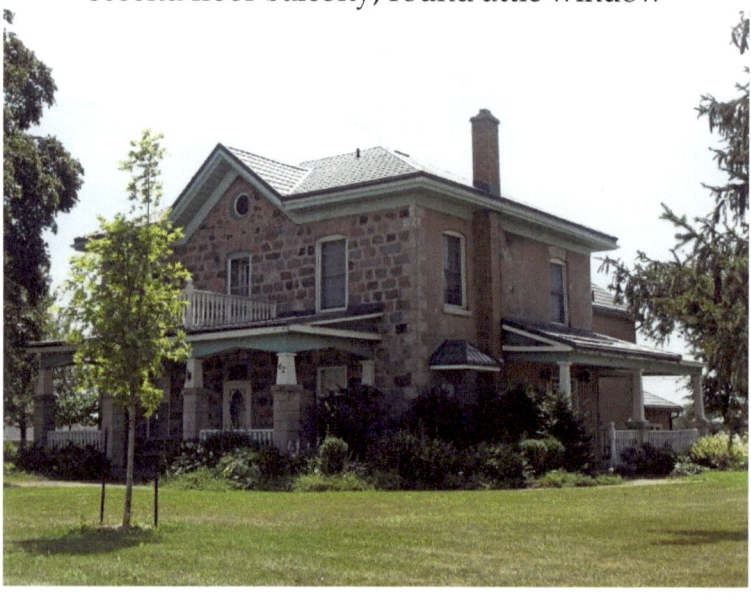

Architectural Terms

Bay Window: A window that projects out from a wall, in a semicircular, rectangular, or polygonal design. Used frequently in Gothic and Victorian designs. Example: 106 Regina Street North, see Page 39	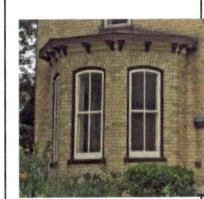
Brackets: a decorative or weight-bearing structural element which forms a right angle with one side against a wall and the other under a projecting surface such as an eave or roof. Example: 33 Scheifele Place, Breslau, Page 57	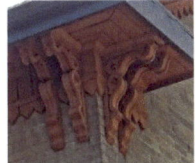
Cobblestone architecture: Refers to the use of cobblestones embedded in mortar as a method for erecting walls on houses and commercial buildings. Example: Woolwich Street, Breslau, Page 48	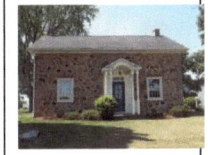
Cornice Return: decorative element on the end of a gable. Example: 33 Scheifele Place, Breslau, Page 57	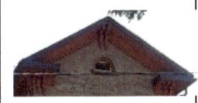
Dormer: (French for "sleep") a gable end window that pierces through the plane of a sloping roof surface to create usable space in the top floor or attic of a building by adding headroom. Example: 53 Alexandra Avenue, Page 30	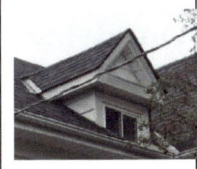

Fretwork: interlaced decorative design resembling a bracket Example: 36 John Street East, Page 14	
Gable: the triangular portion of a wall between the edges of a sloping roof. Example: 49 Menno Street, Page 34	
Iron Cresting: A decorative ornament along the top of a roof. Iron cresting was popular in the Baroque era and also in Italianate, Victorian, Second Empire and Queen Anne styles of architecture. Example: 15 Euclid Avenue, Pg. 23	
Keystones and Voussoirs: a voussoir is a wedge-shaped element used in building an arch. A keystone is the central stone that locks all the stones into position, allowing the arch to bear weight. A keystone is often enlarged and embellished. Voussoir Example: 107 Regina Street North, Page 40	
Oriel Window: These small areas were originally set into walls and galleries for the purpose of private prayer. Over time, any projecting window or area on an upper floor was called an oriel. Example: 90 Moore Avenue South, see Page 44	

Pediment: a triangular section above the horizontal structure (entablature), typically supported by columns. The inside of the triangle is called the tympanum. Example: 90 Moore Avenue South, Page 46	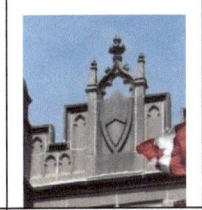
Quoin: masonry blocks at the corner of a wall, often a decorative feature, usually larger or of a different colour than the rest of the wall. Example: 68 Woolwich Street, Breslau, Page 55	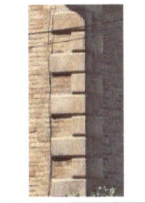
Turret: a small tower that projects from the wall of a building. Example: 90 Moore Avenue South, Page 46	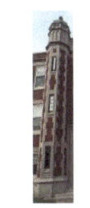
Vergeboard and Finial: also called bargeboards – hang from the projecting end of a roof and are often elaborately carved and ornamented. **Finial:** ornament added to the top of a gable, pinnacle, canopy or spire – a Gothic element. Example: 74 Regina Street North, Page 36	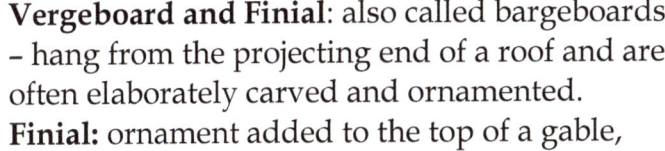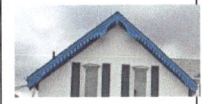

Edwardian, 1900-1930 – This style bridges the ornate and elaborate styles of the Victorian era and the simplified styles of the 20th century. Balanced facades, simple roof lines, dormer windows, large front porches, and smooth brick surfaces are its characteristics. Example: 37 John Street East, Page 14	
Georgian, before 1860 – This style began with the British King Georges in the 18th century. These buildings have balanced facades around a central door, medium-pitched gable roofs, and small paned windows. Example: 20 Menno Street, Page 34	
Gothic Revival, 1830-1890 – These decorative buildings have sharply-pitched gables with highly detailed verge boards, pointed-arch window openings, and dichromatic brickwork. It is a common style in Ontario. Example: 15 Noecker Street, Page 42	
Italianate, 1850-1900 – It has wide-bracketed eaves, belvederes, wrap-around verandahs. Example: 33 Scheifele Place, Breslau, Page 57	

Queen Anne, 1885-1900 – This style is distinguished by an irregular outline featuring a combination of an offset tower, broad gables, projecting two-storey bays, verandahs, multi-sloped roofs, and tall, decorative chimneys. A mixture of brick and wood is common. Windows often have one large single-paned bottom sash and small panes in the upper sash. Example: 56 Euclid Avenue, Page 26	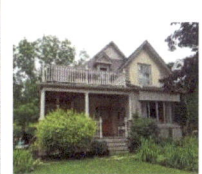
Romanesque Revival, 1880-1910 – This style hearkens back to medieval architecture of the 11th and 12th centuries with a heavy appearance, blocky towers and rounded arches. Example: 48 Alexandra Avenue, Page 31	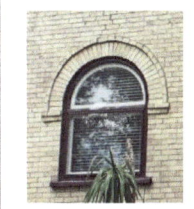
Tudor Revival – exposed timbers with stucco infill, multi-paned windows. Example: 67 Alexandra Avenue, Page 32	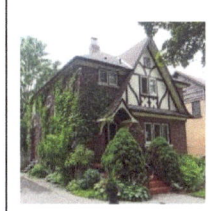
Vernacular/Traditional Mode 1638 - 1950 Influenced but not defined by a particular style, vernacular buildings are made from easily available materials and exhibit local design characteristics. Example: 40 Euclid Avenue, Page 25	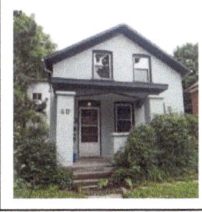